WAIT....WHAT!? THAT'S NOT WHAT I MEANT

A DISCUSSION OF INTERPERSONAL COMMUNICATION

CRYSTAL L. ETZEL, PH.D.

CONTRIBUTING AUTHORS:

KAREN HARRISON, MA

FAIRLIE FIRARI, PH.D.

BENJAMIN MILLER, MA

Kendall Hunt
publishing company

Table of Contents

Chapter 1

"Our lives are defined by opportunities. Even the ones we miss."
—Benjamin Button, *The Curious Case of Benjamin Button*

A Discussion of the Basics

© Doglikehorse/Shutterstock.com

How many decisions did you make before you came to class today? How many of these questions did you ask yourself?

- Should I get up or hit the snooze button?
- What should I wear?
- Should I have breakfast? If yes,
- What should I have for breakfast?
- Will I go to class today?

And that is just a start. We will ask many more questions than these before we make it to the front door. The answer to each of these questions is a choice you will make. Once made other choices are precluded. You then live with the consequences of the choices you made. This is how communication works.

- You make choices.
- You use those choices to send messages.

Communicating effectively is all about the choices we make. You want people to understand you and so you make choices in the hopes that those choices will be the correct ones and that the message you *intend* to send is the message that *is* received. Think about all the decisions you will make in one communication encounter. A sample:

- What language will you use?
- What tone of voice you will use?
- Will you stand or sit?
- How close you will stand to the other person?
- What will you wear?
- Where will you communicate?
- Will you write, phone, fax, tweet, text, Instagram, Tumblr, Snap Chat, voice mail, email, or meet face-to-face?

We call these things rhetorical strategies and we use them all the time without even knowing it. We use them because we subconsciously understand the purpose of communication is.

TO EXCHANGE MEANING

The reason you continually make bad choices is why communication is so difficult. Some individuals might think that communication is common sense or an easy skill, but it is more complex than that. Consider the number of times that you have found yourself in a quarrel that ends with "Yes you did," and "No I didn't," and then tell me you think communication is easy.

If you don't want any more of *those* kinds of conversations, you need to acquire the skills to help you make good choices more often than you make bad ones.

THERE ARE NO GUARANTEES IN COMMUNICATION

© William Perugini/Shutterstock.com

There are no guarantees in communication. Even the best choices sometimes don't work. But learning how to make communication choices will

- Help you to understand why the communication failed.
- Help you to understand the barriers to communication and how to overcome them.
- Help you to understand your perceptions and yourself and how those influences the success or failure of your communication.

Where to begin? Well, definitions are always helpful. But they are only helpful if everyone has the same definition and is working from it. You will find two questions on the next page. Think about them and then give you answer.

THE DEFINITION OF COMMUNICATION

© Gustavo Frazao/Shutterstock.com

What are the different ways in which you communicate? Answer here:

- texting
- social media
- face-to-face
- facetime

If you looked up "communication" in the dictionary what would it say? Answer here. Now add your personal definition of communication.

the imparting or exchanging of information or news.

a connection between places or people.

Since we all had somewhat different definitions, you can see that we have a problem. Unless we are all talking about the same thing, we cannot communicate. Let's gather up our definitions and come to some consensus.

    What are the most important elements in any communication situation? Look at this picture. What do you see?

You see the three important elements that must be present for effective communication to take place:

- Process
- Meaning
- Relationship

Let's break this down so it makes more sense.

Process

Communication continues until meaning is exchanged or we all give up and go home.

The process requires that both parties to the communication work together to make meaning happen. It is not solely the responsibility of the person sending the message. The one receiving the message also has a responsibility to help meaning along.

© LovArt/Shutterstock.com

Meaning

If you don't understand what someone is saying to you for whatever reason, you are not communicating.

If you misunderstand someone's nonverbal cue, you are not communicating.

You are not communicating successfully. You may receive a message, but if it is not the message intended you have not communicated. Communication occurs **only** when both parties in the situation are convinced that they have understood each other.

© Vladimir Mucibabic/Shutterstock.com

Relationship

The act of communicating is the act of relating to another. The better your communication, the better your relationships.

The importance of making the right choices in communication is highlighted by the need to have good relationships with others.

Which brings us to this definition of effective communication.

© Rawpixel.com/Shutterstock.com

Communication is the process by which we exchange meaning in a relationship.

AND NOW A DISCUSSION ABOUT INTERPERSONAL COMMUNICATION

How important are your friendships with family and friends? Consider that you were isolated in a room by yourself. You have no cell phone or any way to connect with anyone! How long could you last without communicating with another individual?

© Catalin Petolea/Shutterstock.com

For many of us, we would not last very long, and that's because interpersonal communication fulfills a variety of needs. Consider the following about interpersonal communication:

- Interpersonal communication improves our health.
- Interpersonal communication develops our identities.
- Interpersonal communication allows us to socialize and build communities.
- Interpersonal communication helps us function in daily personal and work tasks.

How does technology impact your relationship? Or even how you begin relationships?

MEET AND MINGLE SCAVENGER HUNT

Objective for this Assignment:

1) Meet your classmates.
2) Begin the process of developing interpersonal relationships.

Directions:

1) Walk around the classroom and introduce yourself to as many individuals as you can within the allotted time.
2) In your conversations, ask each person ONE of the following questions in the chart.
3) Complete the chart below by writing down that individual's name and the answer they provide.

Name:	Name:
What was your first job?	What high school did you attend?

Name: What type of pet do you have?	Name: What type of car do you have?
Name: What is your favorite TV show?	Name: Who is your best friend?
Name: Where do you want to go for vacation?	Name: What is your favorite meal?

Is there someone that you met that you would want to talk more with? Why is that? This is the beginning of the interpersonal communication and how relationships are formed.

Think back to when you were in elementary school. Why did you hang out with certain individuals? Was it because you were in the same class, or was it because you were next-door neighbors? Proximity has a lot to do with interpersonal relationships, and we will explore this more in later chapters.

THE COMMUNICATION SETTING

To make good choices about how you will communicate you need to know where you will be communicating. Every communication situation is different and requires different skills. Here are the major communication settings you will encounter in your life. These are general categories. We will discuss specific communication situations later. And while this book deals with only one of these, but you should know all of them. It helps.

© Rawpixel.com/Shutterstock.com

Intrapersonal Communication

You communicate with yourself.

- You are probably the first person you talk to in the morning.
- Examples: Questions about when to get up, what to wear, and what to have for breakfast.
- Helps you get to know yourself.
- Helps you solve problems.

© Bogdan Dimofte/Shutterstock.com

Interpersonal Communication

You communicate with others.

- You do this to form a shared meaning.
- You do this to build and maintain relationships.

© Olesia Bilkei/Shutterstock.com

Small Group Communication

You communicate with three or more people for a set purpose.

- Problem-solve, generate information, and debate.
- Team building.

Organizational Communication

You communicate in a business and professional context.

- Systems
- Chain of command
- Formalized

"boxes inside of boxes"

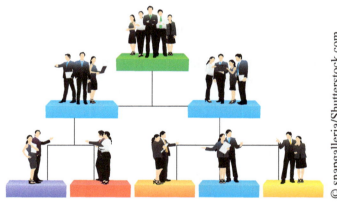

Public Speaking

You communicate with a large group.

- Formal setting
- Prescribed skills
- Public venues

Intercultural Communication

You communicate with culturally diverse people.

- Cannot be separated from the other settings.
- Influences all other settings.

© szefei/Shutterstock.com

Mass Communication

You communicate using media.

- Radio, TV, movies, and YouTube.
- Can be highly impersonal.

© ibreakstock/Shutterstock.com

Computer Mediated Communication

You communicate using social media.

- Facebook, Snap Chat, Tumblr, and texting all have some aspects of Interpersonal Communication.

© quka/Shutterstock.com

INTERPERSONAL COMMUNICATION BASICS

Here are some basic overarching principles of interpersonal communication you need to know. These principles affect everything else, we will talk about these in this class. Learning them now will help you as you navigate the rest of the chapters. Here we go.

© Photographee.eu/Shutterstock.com

Communication = Relationship

No communication. No relationship. You must be in contact in some way with people if you are to be in relationship with them.

The type and amount of communication you engage in with a person defines your relationship with that person.

Important skill: Knowing what kind of relationships you have and responding accordingly.

© Jacob Lund/Shutterstock.com

You are always Communicating

Communication is a 24/7/365 activity. Even when you are asleep you are communicating.

That makes communication continuous. Think of it as always being "on."

Important skill: Because you are always on you need to become more aware of your verbal and nonverbal cues. Learning to control them to the best of your ability will help you be a better communicator.

© Rawpixel.com/Shutterstock.com

You are what you Mean

Language is both universal and specific. Cultures agree on what words and symbols mean. You give your specific meaning to those same words. So words have both general and personal meanings.

Nonverbal cues mean different things to different people.

Important skill: Probe for what people mean by what they say and do.

© Maksim Shirkov/Shutterstock.com

You can't take it back

Communication is irreversible. Once something is said or done that thing will become part of the relationship from then on out.

You have communication history with people. That history makes up the relationship you have with that person.

Important skill: Think before you communicate.

© India Pictures/Shutterstock.com

Messages are two-fold: Content and Emotion

Every message has two components. One is the surface message, the content of the message. "Let's go to the movies."

Then there is the underlying message, the emotional message, "we don't do things together anymore."

The emotional message, as you can tell from this example, is not always clear.

Your job as a communicator is to figure out what both messages are relying to you.

Important skill: Learn which one to respond to and respond to it.

© TraXXe/Shutterstock.com

Practice Makes Permanent

Communication skills are learned. We are not born skilled communicators. Just like these hip-hop artists need practice to perfect their craft, you need to study how you communicate and enhance what works, and dump what doesn't.

Important skill: Practice, practice, and practice.

© Lucky Business/Shutterstock.com

There are Rules

In relationships, people make rules about how they will communicate.

These rules are the do's and don'ts for specific people and situations.

All relationships have these rules. No two relationships have the same set of rules. That is why you end up in fights with your roommates. You bring your rules from home to your new living situation.

Important skill: Learn what these are and use them.

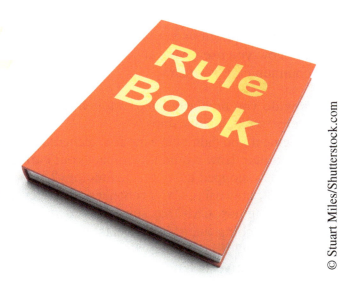

© Stuart Miles/Shutterstock.com

Sometimes the best communication is no communication

More communication is not necessarily better communication. There is a time to talk and a time to be quiet. There is a time to do and a time to, as Yoda would say, do not.

Important skill: Learn to know the difference.

© Vladimir Gjorgiev/Shutterstock.com

Discussion Activity 1: #MeanTweets and CMC

Learning Objectives for this Assignment:

1) Consider your use of Computer Mediated Communication (CMC), and how it affects your relationships.
2) Become aware of the communication you post using CMC, and whether it strengthens or hurts your relationships.
3) Identify appropriate and inappropriate uses of CMC, and analyze how it impacts your interpersonal communication.

Video Clip:

Before you begin, watch Jimmy Kimmel's #MeanTweets and think about information that you have posted online.

https://www.youtube.com/watch?v=LsKFsF2zpFM

Directions:

The following questions are meant for you to answer independently, and then share with a group. Explore how you use CMC, and how technology impacts your interpersonal relationships and how you communicate in general.

1) How do you regularly keep in touch with friends and family? Are you able to maintain those interpersonal relationships?
2) Imagine if you didn't have modern technology, such as your cell phone, FaceTime, Skype, or even a computer. How would this impact your current relationships? What would happen if someone you knew stopped using this technology?
3) Consider how using CMC enhances your interpersonal relationships. Write down three examples explaining how CMC has strengthened your relationships.
4) After watching the #MeanTweets, does CMC has any negative impacts on interpersonal communication? What are they?
5) What negative behaviors might you change so that you can improve your interpersonal relationships?

Name: _____

Introduction Speeches
25 POINTS

Directions: You will work along with a peer in this course and introduce them to the class. Your goal is to effectively communicate the necessary information to the class, and have fun and successful experience with your first speech.

You will earn points for introducing your classmate, telling us three things you have in common with each other, and telling a specific story. The story can be about an event that recently happened, or it could be a story from when they were younger. You must make eye contact with the class, and display energy and enthusiasm to earn maximum points for this speech.

Have fun! Remember, the story you tell the class should be class-appropriate.

Rubric:

States Full Name: _____ / 2 Point
States three Commonalities: _____ / 5 Points
Tells a Coherent Story: _____ / 5 Points
Energy and Enthusiasm: _____ / 3 Points
Eye Contact with Audience: _____ / 5 Points
30 Second Time Minimum: _____ / 5 Points
_____

Total Points Earned: _____ **/ 25 Points**

Additional Comments:

Chapter 2

"What we've got here is a failure to communicate"

—The Captain, *Cool Hand Luke*

A Discussion of the Communication Model

Every communication encounter you have will be a unique event. However, there are some features that are present in every one of them. Knowing what are these features is essential for effective communication. And that is why we are going to look at Communication Theory right now.

Why you need to know communication theory.

- You need to look at basic communication theory because what it tells you has a direct impact on the choices you make while communicating.
- It is also important to know because you are continually engaged in communication and you ought to be able to see what is going on around you and give it a name.
- Once you name and define a thing, you can begin to understand and control it.

All effective communication is transactional. That is what is meant by the definition: **Communication is a process by which we exchange meaning in a relationship**. The process requires a back and forth among the participants for

- Meaning to be exchanged.
- Relationships to be built and/or maintained.

What you are about to encounter is a pictorial representation of what happens every time you communicate. The picture will contain all the elements that occur—the universals of communication—every time communication happens. In communication theory, this picture is called the Communication Model. Many communication scholars design their own models, so there are lots of them out there. Generally, the models contain the same things. They might be called by different names, but basically the pictures represent the same things. By the end of this discussion, you will be able to create your own model, one that will include all the important aspects of the communication situation.

THE COMMUNICATION SUPER MODEL

The communication model has seven parts. These are not the same on every model. You will see them represented in different ways and with a variety of names. This is the terminology we will use:

© Nadezhda79/Shutterstock.com

- Context
- Sender
- Channel
- Message
- Receiver
- Feedback
- Noise

We are going to look at these elements as discrete entities. We must because that is how paper and ink work. In real life, these elements will be happening at once. Keep that in mind as we plow through them.

CONTEXT

All communication takes place in a given arena or context. The context has four essential elements:

- Physical
- Cultural
- Social-Psychological
- Temporal

These elements are present in every communication context and influence it in a variety of ways. The choices **you** make in each context are also affected by these four elements. Here is how you might think about these elements as you make your communication choices.

Physical Context

The actual space in which the communication takes place. Examples:

- Classroom
- Stadium
- Bar
- Restaurant
- Home

The picture here suggests a large room with enthusiastic people. You could probably get these people to sing and dance to "YMCA." They are out having fun in a big space where jumping up and down and yelling are acceptable. Would you stand up and sing the "YMCA" song here in this classroom? Spontaneously? If your grade depended on it?

Cultural Context

The norms, roles, rules, and patterns of behavior that speakers and listeners bring to the communication situation constitute the cultural context. Examples include:

- Expectations
- Rules of behavior
- Dress
- Vocal cues
- Spatial considerations (how close you stand to someone)
- Eye contact

This context also includes:

- Formal or informal considerations. Is this a formal occasion? Are you there to have fun?
- The occasion. Graduation Party. 21ˢᵗ Birthday night out. Funeral.

An example of this element is classroom behavior. You have been taught how to behave in a classroom and you behave that way until told otherwise.

- Sitting in rows
- Raising hands
- Word-processed work

When you were in elementary school did you stand up when your teacher came into the room and remain standing until told to sit? No? Yes? If you answered "no" then you probably did the bulk of your schooling in the United States. In many places in the world, children are required to stand when their teachers enter the room.

Social-Psychological Context

The context of any communication situation includes aspects of authority, status, power, and the nature of the relationship among the communicants and the climate—friendly or unfriendly
formal or informal
comfortable or uncomfortable.

Every relationship is characterized by authority, status, and power considerations. Who has authority, status, and power in the photograph? It's the king, of course. Notice that the queen is sitting below him and the knights are standing. Those cues indicate who has the authority, status, and power in this context.

The climate of any given communication context is highly influenced by the power structure in that context. The lawyer sits behind the desk, back to the window and you sit across with the sun shining in your eyes. Who has the power? How do you respond?

Temporal Context

The time of day in which your communication takes place is important. You think and act differently at 8 am than you do at 8 pm. More importantly, you think and act differently at 2 pm than you do at 2 am.

(Cow-tipping) at 2 am seemed like such a good idea and such fun at the time, but when the cops come the next morning to ask you about it doesn't seem like such a good idea after all. (If you don't know what this is ask a friend who grew up in the country.)

© tomertu/Shutterstock.com

Your history within a given context is also a consideration. If you have been successful in a classroom in the past, you are likely to bring that sense of success with you to every classroom.

A secondary history consideration is where the message fits into the sequence of events. Are you the first to communicate in the context? Are you responding to a message?

CONTEXT EXERCISE

Using the elements of the context discussed above, describe the communication context in your classroom.

Physical

classroom

Cultural

expectations, how we dress, spatial considerations

Social-Psychological

Temporal

Use this inventory to discuss how this context might affect your communication success in this place.

THE SENDER

This is the person in the communication situation who sends the first message. The sender, also known as

- Encoder
- Speaker
- Source
- Sender or Receiver (to indicate the process), is a unique source.

Each sender has personal beliefs, attitudes, values, behaviors, and experiences that make up who that person is.

Your beliefs, attitudes, values, behaviors, and experiences make up not just who you are. They influence what you communicate and how you choose to do it—your BAVBE—. For example, your experiences in a classroom affect how you communicate in subsequent classes. If you felt comfortable in class and believed yourself to be successful, then you will bring a certain confidence with you to every other class.

You are your message. Your BAVBE are the building block with which you formulate and transmit your message. In fact, your BAVBE influence every part of the model.

- Context—former experiences in the context
- Channel—if I am not tech savvy then no Snapchat for me
- Message—my nonverbal cues are influenced by
    - ❑ Culture
    - ❑ Family
    - ❑ Education

© Uber Images/Shutterstock.com

The words I choose are taken from my vocabulary, which has been highly influenced by
  ❏ Books
  ❏ Movies
  ❏ Area of study
  ❏ Geography
- Listener—experience with this listener. Attitudes toward the listener
- Feedback—see message
- Noise—what affects me and what doesn't internally and externally

BAVBE INVENTORY

Jot down one or two examples for each of the categories.

I hold these beliefs: (for example: people are created good; the Earth is flat.)

My Attitudes about the following are: (for example: I like Pepsi better than Coke.)

the pittsburgh penguins are trash.

I hold these values: (for example: loyalty is important; it is OK to cheat on a test.)

if someone is being rude to you its perfectly ok to act the same way back.

I engage in these behaviors: (for example: like I try to be funny everywhere I am.)

i try to be understanding even when people are being obnoxious and extra.

I have had these experiences: (choose something like the most fun thing you ever did or the experience that had the biggest effect on your life.)

going to toronto.

An exercise like this will help you understand how your messages are shaped.

THE MESSAGE

Messages have two components:

- The actual surface content.
- The feelings or emotions underlying that content.

As a sender, you need to be aware of both components and make clear, which component requires a response. You may not be aware of which component is most important to you and that can be a problem. If you don't know which component needs a response how can the listener know that?

Messages can be verbal, nonverbal, or both. They consist of that idea, belief, attitude, and value that you wish the other party in the situation to understand.

SOME THINGS TO KNOW ABOUT MESSAGES

Messaging occurs simultaneously

You are receiving messages from the listener at the same time you are sending your message. That's the feedback loop that makes communication transactional.

You must be aware of the messages being sent to you and respond to them as you send your message. An example would be your professor acknowledging your raised hand with a nod as the lecture continues.

That nod tells you that your professor knows you want to respond and will call on you at the appropriate time.

Messages are here to stay

Once words are spoken they are there for eternity. People will remember them even if they say they won't.

These words become part of the context in which you communicate with this person from then on. They will affect future communication.

Messages are who you are

Remember that your messages are comprised of your BAVBE. You bring your own history to every message you send.

You bring your perceptions of the world around you to every message you send, too. Your perceptions of the world are not the same as the listener's perceptions. This is one of the difficulties of communication that needs to be overcome for meaning to be exchanged.

© file404/Shutterstock.com

Messages are influenced by context

You ask, "How are you?" when you greet a friend on the street. You are expecting, "Fine. How are you?" not a rundown of that friend's medical condition. If this exchange took place in a hospital room, you would expect the medical details.

© chrisitzeimaging.com/Shutterstock.com

MESSAGES EXERCISE

Jot down a few thoughts about the following. Discussion will happen.

The worst thing someone ever said to me was:
   I was _____ years old when this happened.

The nicest thing someone ever said to me was:
   I was _____ years old when this happened.

I remember these things because:

CHANNEL

The channel is the way the message is sent. It is not the message itself. It is the sender's responsibility to choose the best channel for the message the sender wishes to convey.

You have so much to choose from here, much more than in the past. The better you make this choice, the better chance you have of exchanging meaning.

A channel can be virtually anything. Here is a not definitive list:

- Cell phone
- Landline phone
- Voicemail
- Text
- Snapchat
- YouTube video
- Face-to-face communication
- Letter
- Sky writing
- Secret decoder ring
- Clothing
- Books

The channel can influence whether the message is received.

CHANNEL EXERCISE

You want to propose to your significant other. You have a choice of channels through which you can send this message. Look at the list above. In your opinion, which channel is best for this message? Which is worst? Jot down some thoughts.

Now, choose three of the channels above and compose a message for each letting your significant other know that you want to spend the rest of your lives together. Look at those messages and reflect on how they might be received.

LISTENER

This is the person/s for whom the message is intended. Your message may be received by many different people. But as a sender you have tailored your message to a specific audience.

Listeners have their own BAVBE. They have their own perceptions. These BAVBE and perceptions are unlikely to be the same as the sender's. It is important for both the sender and the listener to understand this. A look back at the discussion about the sender is helpful as all that information applies here.

The Listener's job is to offer feedback to the sender. Feedback is essentially the listener's message to the sender. Through feedback, the listener lets the sender know how the listener understands the message.

The listener has choices to make:

© Javier Brosch/Shutterstock.com

■ What channel will I use?
■ What type of feedback will be most effective?

FEEDBACK

Feedback is the message that the listener sends to the sender. This can be and usually is both verbal and nonverbal. Feedback alerts the sender of the listener's understanding of the message. The listener indicates how the message was received. It is now up to the sender to decide if the listener got it.

Feedback comes is a variety of dyads. Here are a few:

© eenevski/Shutterstock.com

Supportive feedback is just what it sounds like. Supportive feedback might be what you do when you are responding to the emotion behind the words and gestures and not the surface meaning.

FEEDBACK REFLECTION

Your friend has asked you to go to a recording session to listen and comment. You don't like the kind of music your friend plays. Plus, you think it will be a boring day. Suggest a feedback response for each of these dyads.

Immediate or Delayed Feedback:

Low monitored or High monitored Feedback:

Critical or Supportive Feedback:

NOISE, ROADBLOCKS, BARRIERS, BREAKDOWNS

This element is the last one we talk about because of its influence on all the other aspects of the model. It is the noise in the channel (as it used to be called) that interferes with meaning exchange. Think of Noise as a virus that attacks your computer. Your iPad, tablet, and laptop become useless and uncommunicative when a virus strikes.

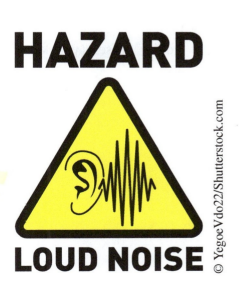

© YegoeVdo22/Shutterstock.com

It's like that for the communication model. Noise interferes with every aspect of communication and can make meaning exchange impossible.

All communication situations have noise. Your job as both sender and listener is to figure out what the noise is and minimize it. Your ability to do this will help you be an effective communicator.

Below are categories of noise.

External Noise / *physical noise*

Anything is the physical context that can interfere with the message.

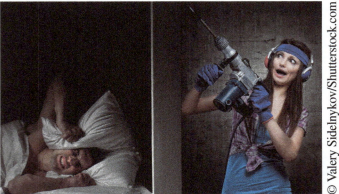

© Valery Sidelnykov/Shutterstock.com

- Lights
- Clocks
- Windows or no windows
- Weather

Just because this part of the model is called noise doesn't mean that the interference is strictly auditory. Look at the list above. You can see that almost anything in the environment can block communication if that thing takes your attention away from the message.

Biological Noise

Any physical problems experienced by either the speaker or the listener that would interfere with the message.

© leungchopan/Shutterstock.com

- Cough
- Cold
- Stomach bug
- Pain
- Bodily noises (you know who you are)

Words

Vocabulary Noise

Any language use by either the speaker or the listener that would interfere with meaning exchange.

- Red or Green flag words
- Jargon
- Slang
- Technical language
- Foreign languages
  - *Terminology*

© ibreakstock/Shutterstock.com

Nonverbal Noise

Any use of nonverbal cues that interferes with meaning exchange.

- Paralanguage: grunts, groans, tone of voice
- Spatial cues
- Clothing
- Artifacts
- Territory

© Luis Molinero/Shutterstock.com

Psychological or Emotional Noise

Emotions or feelings experienced by speaker or listener that interfere with the exchange of meaning.

- Happy or sad
- Sarcasm
- Angry
- Cynical
- Joyful
- Contented

© g-stockstudio/Shutterstock.com

Relational Noise

Any authority, status, and power in the relationship that might interfere with communication.

- Exes (any and all types of)
- Teacher or student
- Famous person or not famous person
- Rich or not rich
- Parent or child
- Employee or customer

Social or Cultural Noise

Any part of your cultural heritage or social upbringing that would cause meaning not to be exchanged.

- Etiquette rules
- Spatial rules
- Relationship rules
- Order of precedence rules (who out ranks whom)

Noise Exercise

You have already jotted down the elements of context that are at play in this room. Now look for noise. List all the things in this room that might prevent you from paying attention and exchanging meaning.

Environmental:

Biological:

Verbal:

Nonverbal:

Psychological or Emotional:

Relational (authority, status, and power):

Social or Cultural:

NOW DRAW THE SUPER MODEL

Now you know all the elements of the model discussed in this chapter. You know that the model represents the process that happens every time we try to communicate. So, here is your chance to be a communication scholar. Use this blank space to design your own model. Make sure it represents the process, the give and take that happens every time you communicate. Include all the elements. Have fun.

Immediate or Delayed Feedback

Immediate Feedback occurs at the time the message is sent. Often this is nonverbal—a nod, a smile, or an involuntary reaction. Immediate feedback can also be a question or a paraphrase of the message.

Delayed Feedback occurs after some time has elapsed between sending and receiving the message. Examples of delayed feedback:

© dkART/Shutterstock.com

- A written response to a letter.
- A movie review in a newspaper.
- A voicemail (when you don't really want to talk to the person but want to say you responded).
- Response to an invitation.

Low monitored or high monitored Feedback

This is the difference between a spontaneous response and a well thought-out formalized response.

- Low Monitoring: spontaneous reaction
- High Monitoring: thought-out reaction

© lipik/Shutterstock.com

Low-monitored spontaneous reactions can be fun, like when you jump out at your friend from behind a door and get the desired response. But spontaneous responses can also be hurtful like when you watch your friend open a present and see the look of disappointment on your friend's face.

It is possible that the sender would perceive a spontaneous response as being more honest because people generally believe you have less control over spontaneous responses. However, people who practice high self-monitoring in all aspects of their lives can make their responses seem spontaneous even when they are not.

Critical or Supportive Feedback

Critical feedback is analytical. You evaluate what you have heard. This is not necessarily a bad thing. If you have someone you trust who can tell you hard truths, then this is exactly the kind of feedback you want.

© A. and I. Kruk/Shutterstock.com

Chapter 3

"I'm big! It's the pictures that got small."

—Norma Desmond, *Sunset Blvd*

A Discussion of Perception

HOOD

List five things this word means to you.

1)
2)
3)
4)
5)

So why did you make these choices? What do your choices say about how you view the world?

They say this: How you perceive the world influences your communication.

Look out the window (if your classroom has one, or you are at home). What does the day look like? Is it

- gloomy or soft
- partly sunny or partly cloudy (yes weather people have a specific definition of these terms but you don't)
- overcast or dreary?

How you describe the weather tells your listener a lot about how you feel about the day and how you respond to external stimuli. Your language choice explains to your listener your outlook. It describes your feelings. It paints a picture of the day for the listener that the listener can agree with or not.

In order to make better communication choices you need to know about perception—yours and other people's—what it is, how it works, and how it influences messaging.

We should start out with a definition. Or in this case two. What is your definition of perception? What does the word mean to you? Try these:

- Perception is **the process of gathering information and giving it meaning.**
- Perception is h**ow you view the world.**

It should not be surprising that perception is a process. So as we did with the communication process we will break down the perception process to see what it is all about.

The purpose of the process is to generate meaning. How you do this is by gathering information.

GATHERING INFORMATION

How do we gather information that will then allow us to generate meaning? We use our senses:

- Hearing
- Sight
- Taste
- Touch
- Smell

Obviously, information comes to you in different ways and at different times and in different

forms. We use our sense of touch to tell if a piece of fruit is ripe. We use our sense of smell to decide if dinner is going to be yummy.

You interpret this information based on the subconscious process of perception, which uses not only your senses, but also all of who you are—your BAVBE (beliefs, attitudes, values, behaviors and experiences). Because you are a unique individual your perceptions of the world will necessarily be different than those of others.

THE PROCESS OF PERCEPTION

Naturally, perception is a process. Everything in communication is. So we will now look at the process of perception. If you know how it works, then you can better understand how and why you are seeing things the way you are.

© sezer66/Shutterstock.com

SELECTIVE ATTENTION

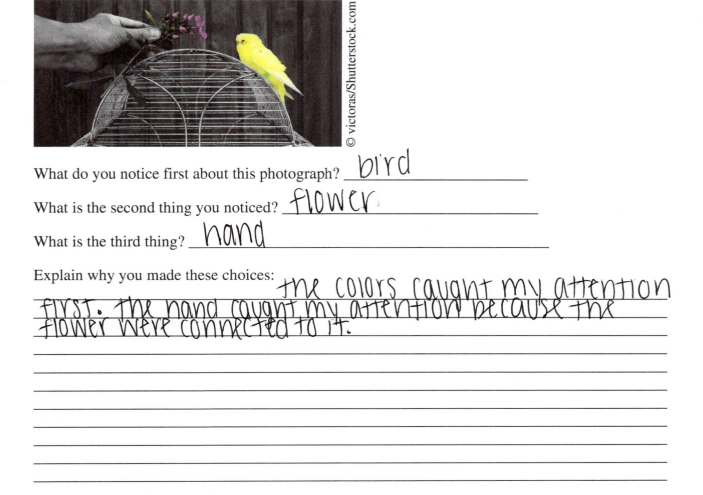

© victoras/Shutterstock.com

What do you notice first about this photograph? ___bird___

What is the second thing you noticed? ___flower___

What is the third thing? ___hand___

Explain why you made these choices: ___the colors caught my attention first. The hand caught my attention because the flower were connected to it.___

Now, did you feel compelled to write enough to fill up all the lines? If so, why? If you did it was because of how you perceived those lines.

- You might have said to yourself "All these blank lines would not be here if I was not expected to fill them in."
- Or you might have said "The publisher is just trying to fill up space."
- Or you might have said, "Those blank lines are just a suggestion, I can do what I want."

Your perception of the blanks and why they are there influence your communication.

Because we are bombarded by so many different stimuli at any given time we need a way to filter things out. We are not the Borg so we cannot possibly assimilate all the information we are given all at once. (If you don't know who the Borg are, ask a friend who is a Star Trek fan.) Our defense mechanism is our ability to attend to some things and remember those and filter out the rest. That is why you "saw" the photo in the "order" you did.

We do this all the time. You do it, for example, in a classroom. You decide what information you think is important and you take it down in your notes. You also, by the way, try to guess what information your instructor thinks is important and therefore what will be on the exam. This is called **selective attention.**

Remember that we filter all stimuli through our senses and our beliefs, attitudes, values, behaviors, and experiences as we try to make sense of the world. Here are a few things that influence that attempt.

INFLUENCES ON SELECTIVE ATTENTION

© Rawpixel.com/Shutterstock.com

Intensity

When we see something out of the ordinary we are likely to focus on that.

- Very tall or very short people do that to us.
- Bright colors.
- Odd shapes.

© Anky/Shutterstock.com

What do you attend to in this video? https://youtu.be/Ahg6qcgoay4

Repetition

We are likely to attend to things that repeat.

- Commercial jingles.
- Dripping water.
- Our parents telling us to take out the garbage.
- Watching a movie dozens of times.

Where do these catch phrases come from?

Go ahead. Make my day. _____

I am the king of the world. _____

I'll be back. _____

May the Force be with you. *Star wars* _____

I have a feeling we're not in Kansas anymore. *Wizard of Oz*

Here's Johnnny! _____

You're going to need a bigger boat. _____

Hello, my name is Inigo Montoya. You killed my father. Prepare to die. _____

To infinity . . . and beyond! *Toy Story* _____

Khaaaaan! _____

How many of these did you recognize? What influenced that recognition? If you did not recognize any of them or only a few, why might that be?

Contrast or Change

You are influenced by a sudden change in visual or auditory stimuli.

A newly painted building on your usual route to school will catch your attention.

A change in a friend's appearance will do that too:

- Loss of weight in a friend.
- Hair piece.
- New tattoo.

TRY THIS

Think about the route you take to school. This works if you walk from the residence halls or drive to the college. Think about what you see. Make a list here:

Now think about something new that suddenly caught your attention as you made your way to class. What was it? Why did you suddenly see "something that was not there?"

What did you see?

What was the change that "forced" you to notice the object?

Motives

Your motives have a lot to do with what you attend to. This influence answers the question "why?" It has to do with the reasons you want to see things in a particular way. Synonyms would be

- Rationale
- Intention
- Purpose

What do you want out of a particular communication situation? Why are you communicating in this situation?

For example, if you are in a bad mood and you want to stay that way, you will selectively attend to every part of your day that re-enforces your desire to stay angry.

We seldom if ever go into a communication situation without some kind of agenda. Other examples:

- Are you eager to have a good time at a party?
- Are you eager to have a bad time at a party?
- Do you not care about the party and want to show that?
- Do you want to please one particular person at that party?
- Do you want to seem part of the crowd?
- Do you want to stand above it all?

The answer to these questions will have you selectively attending to the stimuli that satisfies that motive.

Look at the photograph below. Then, using information gleaned from the photo, fill in the box.

If I want to have a good time I will selectively attend to:	If I want to have a not so good time I will selectively attend to:

Interests

You attend to what you are interested in.

If you are uninterested in cars, it is unlikely that you would click on or even notice the *Top Gear* Netflix option, see the *Car and Driver* magazine on the table at the doctor's office, or focus on the cars in the *Fast and Furious* franchise.

Movies are a good example of how this influence works. A movie is successful or not **for you** based on what your focus is—what interests you. If you are an action-oriented viewer, you are going to attend mostly to the action. The lack of compelling dialog will probably not be factored into your thumbs up for the film. If you are interested in costuming and know something about it, you will give a thumbs down to a costume drama others might like because the 18th century dresses have zippers up the back.

© Whitevector/Shutterstock.com

Wants and/ or Needs

You attend to those things that meet your immediate needs. For example

- Hunger
- Security
- Fulfillment
- Belonging

© pathdoc/Shutterstock.com

Here is a scenario for you. Your car is about to give up. You need a new one. What happens?

- You begin noticing makes and models of cars as you drive.
- You begin reading the car advertisements.
- You begin listening and attending to conversations about cars.

When you have finally purchase your new car, you stop doing all these things. Unless of course you continue these activities because you have a general interest in cars.

You are late for an appointment. You are driving to this appointment. What items in your surroundings will you pay most attention to? Jot down five possibilities.

1)

2)

3)

4)

5)

Culture

Your perceptions are influenced by the culture in which you live, as well as the cultures from which you come. Those influences include:

- Norms
- Rules
- Behaviors
- Artifacts

© Rawpixel.com/Shutterstock.com

We are influenced to attend to some things and not others as those things either re-enforce or contradict our cultures. For example, you might perceive your friend as coming from a family with no understanding of manners if the friend

- wears shoes in the house,
- sets the table differently than you, or
- hangs the toilet paper so it unrolls under the roll.

The rules of conduct in the home in which you grew up makes you attend to these things.

Or you come from a culture where the signifier for marriage is a ring on the **RIGHT** hand. You selectively attend to the absence of a ring on the right and approach a potential date. You get told off because you didn't attend to the ring on the left ring finger. Really, you couldn't because you didn't even know you needed to.

YOU AND YOUR ROOMMATE

Make a list of the cultural norms, rules, artifacts you brought to a roommate/live in/marriage situation. Then, as best you can, make the same list for your roommate/live in/marriage partner.

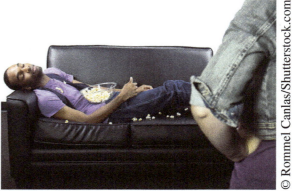

© Rommel Canlas/Shutterstock.com

How might these things influence your perception of your roommate/live in/marriage partner?

ORGANIZATION

In order to be able to communicate what we have attended to, we have to organize the information. We have to choose how to organize the material and naturally our choices are based on our perception. How we organize this information will influence the final step in the process. Organization is a choice we make. If we choose well communication is more likely to take place.

Here are some examples of how we organize information.

© Rawpixel.com/Shutterstock.com

Similarity

We organize material based on similar characteristics.

- Library books
- Grocery Store shelves
- Retail store clothing racks

In this photo, the umbrellas can be organized by what they are "umbrellas" or their color "rainbow." The point is that they are similar in various ways. So we interpret this picture as showing multi-colored umbrellas.

© Sanit Fuangnakhon/Shutterstock.com

Proximity

Proximity simply means how close things are to each other as they inhabit space. When we see people sitting together we naturally assume that these people know one another and have a connection somehow even though they may be total strangers.

Look at the photo. We assume because the cars are parked in this MacDonald's parking lot that the cars "belong" to MacDonald's. That is more than likely, but there is always a chance that someone parked in this lot and is patronizing the business next door.

© Felix Mizioznikov/Shutterstock.com

Perceptions

You organize information based on how you understand it.

© pathdoc/Shutterstock.com

Let's do an exercise.

Who do You Organize this Information?
  BAKER'S JOY

Baker's Joy is a spray oil that contains flour. Its purpose is to make life easier for bakers. Instead of having to grease a pan and then flour it, Baker's Joy does these two steps in one. By shaking the can and then straying the pan, both oil and flour are deposited on the pan at the same time. It contains zero calories.

You work in a grocery store. Where would you shelve this product? With the

- ☑ Spray Oils
- ❏ Flour
- ❏ Diet Products
- ❏ Other:_____

Why did you make your choice?
  that's literally what it is.

Schemata

Schemata are ways you think about things in general.

They are how you organize information based on notions that you hold.

They are unconscious in many ways because they are unexamined assumptions about how life works. Schemata come in four flavors: Prototypes, Personal Constructs, Stereotypes or Predictive Generalizations, and Scripts

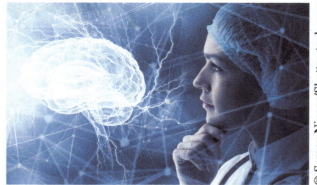

© Sergey Nivens/Shutterstock.com

Prototypes

Look at this lovely house. Is this your idea of "house?" Is this the best example of what most represents this category to you?

You have decided for yourself what best exemplifies people, places, or things. These are your prototypes and you judge the world on a scale of the best to the worst exemplar of the category.

All those online lists of the best 100 movies, or top 100 songs of all time or most attractive star are all lists based on prototypes.

© Anna Tamila/Shutterstock.com

EXERCISE YOUR PROTOTYPES

Take five minutes and list the characteristics that the BEST representative of each category must have.

An example: Action hero. The best prototype action hero is strong, brave, funny, cool under fire. This hero either has a secret or a haunted past and of course a catch phrase.

Teacher:

Best Friend:

Romantic Interest:

Now break up into groups and share your lists. What do they have in common? Combine your lists and be ready to discuss.

Personal Constructs

Personal constructs are used to judge people, places, and things on a scale from best to worst.

We ask how smart, nice, attractive someone is and then we place them on our personal scale. These constructs help us narrow our focus to specific categories.

We decide for ourselves who we consider attractive, what foods are best or worst, what movies we like or don't based on our personal scale of best to worst.

© EgudinKa/Shutterstock.com

EXERCISING YOUR PERSONAL CONSTRUCTS

Place a mark on the scale. In one sentence justify your answer. Be prepared to share.

© Valua Vitaly/Shutterstock.com

Attractive_____|_____Unattractive

Scary _____|_____Not scary   Best Cuisine_____|Worst Cuisine

Stereotyping or Predictive Generalizations

Stereotypes are predictive generalizations and in their purest form are nothing more than a tool we use to predict how someone will behave or what will happen in a certain situation.

Predictive generalizations are essentially a defense mechanism. They are a starting point for assessing the communication potential in any given situation. Stereotypes or Predictive generalizations can be accurate or inaccurate. The more accurate they are the more likely effective communication will take place.

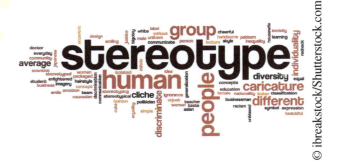

EXERCISING YOUR PREDICTIVE GENERALIZATIONS

Describe the typical College Student:

In what ways does your answer describe you? In which ways does it not?

Pair up with a classmate. Share your list. How closely do the characteristics of your classmate conform to your Predictive Generalizations?

Scripts

This is another way of talking about expectations.

Your expectations are based on your experiences, how you were brought up, and your culture among other things.

You have an idea of what "should" happen in any given situation. You organize material based on how people "should" react in that situation.

An example of a cultural script is how we greet one another in the street. For example, Klingons greet one another with the question "What do you want?" In America, nonKlingons greet one another with the question "How are you?". (If you don't know who the Klingons are ask a friend who is Star Trek fan.)

An example of a family script is, "We are frugal people. We are careful with our money."

EXERCISING YOUR SCRIPTS

List three cultural scripts you use in everyday life.

List three family scripts you use in everyday life.

Partner with a classmate and share these scripts.

How are they the same? How are they different?

INTERPRETATION

It is at this stage in the process that we tell people what we believe is going on in a given communication situation. We assign meaning to the information we gathered and organized and then send our message.

- We explain how we view the world to those around us.
- Our message is our perception.

What are you attending to when looking at this picture? How are you organizing the material you see? What is your interpretation of this image?

© Photo/Shutterstock.com

INFLUENCES ON OUR PERCEPTIONS

Who you are as a person has a profound influence on your perceptions. Knowing what influences you to see the world the way you do helps you become a more effective communicator. Here are some of the factors that influence your view of the world.

INFLUENCE

© Alfa Photo/Shutterstock.com

Past Experiences

We are likely to interpret similar situations in a similar way. If we had one bad experience at a sporting event, we may interpret all elements of the next event negatively.

A negative experience in a classroom might encourage you to interpret other classrooms in a negative light.

© Michaela Stejskalova/Shutterstock.com

Assumptions about Human Behavior

What we believe about human nature will affect how we interpret behavior. This is the old nature or nurture debate.

■ People are born that way (nature).
■ People are taught (nurture).

Are people born good or evil **or** do they become good or evil? Are people born selfish or unselfish? Are people born cruel or kind? How you answer these and many other questions will influence how you view the world.

© Vlue/Shutterstock.com

Look at these two sentences:

■ People generally do as little as possible to get by.
■ People generally try to do their best.

Which one of these is closest to how you think people generally behave? Why do you think that?

Depending on which one of these assumptions you believe you will treat the customer service representative as unhelpful or as doing the best a customer representative can do.

Expectations

We perceive what we expect to perceive. This is why it is always a shock when we see people from home when we are on vacation.

Or think about this:

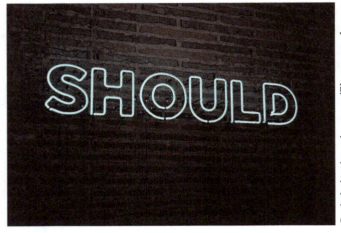

© chrisitzeimaging.com/Shutterstock.com

It's your birthday. What should happen on your birthday? Write down a couple of things.

Now, why do you think these things should happen?

What was your response when those things did not happen?

Emotion

You will perceive situations through the emotions you feel at any given time. If you are happy then that happiness will encourage you to see the world as a bright and entertaining place. If you are sad then even the sun has a dreary aspect to it.

Your emotional state influences all three parts of the perception process, by the way.

An example of how emotions shape our perceptions is close calls in sports. If the umpire makes a close call in favor of your team you rejoice. If the call is made against you the umpire needs glasses and should be fired.

© Kues/Shutterstock.com

Language

How we label things has a powerful effect on how we perceive them. If that were not true, then companies would not spend so much time and money naming their products.

Parents would not spend so much time choosing names for their children if they didn't think it meant something.

And you wouldn't have so many names by which you are known if language and perception were not so entwined.

You have designed a sports car. What will you name it? Why?

© VikaSuh/Shutterstock.com

You are about to open a restaurant. What will you name it?

You wish to invent a new insult to call people you don't like. What is it?

Attitudes, Beliefs, and Values

Our beliefs, attitudes, and values influence perception.

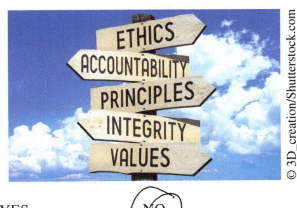

© 3D_creation/Shutterstock.com

- Think of various political debates. Where you stand on issues and how you perceive those who don't agree with you are influenced by your beliefs, attitudes, and values.
- It is this influence that makes it so difficult to listen to people with whom we disagree.

Should college athletes be paid to play?   YES   NO⃝

Give three reasons why you answered the way you did.

- it's just school
- you don't get paid to go to school
- it's not the pro's so they are not *that* good.

What beliefs, attitudes, and values are illustrated by your answer?

Why do you have these beliefs, attitudes, and values?

Primacy or Recency

Primacy refers to first impressions. We tend to be influenced by what we first encounter. Malcolm Gladwell's book "Blink" is a good resource for this phenomenon.

Recency refers to last impressions. We tend to be influenced by the last thing we see or hear, touch or taste, or smell.

Likely you are one or the other. You should know if you are a primacy person—someone who is most influenced first impressions—or a recency person—someone who is most influenced by that last thing you encounter. Knowing this about yourself will help guard you against a narrow perception of the world.

© Constantin Stanciu/Shutterstock.com

Perspective

How close or far away you are from something can influence how you see it.

From a distance trees can look like people.

Forced perspective in movies make actors look taller than they are. Here is a list of actors and their heights. What here surprises you?

© Annette Shaff/Shutterstock.com

Actor	Height in Feet and Inches
Zac Efron	5'6
Jet Li	5'6
Tom Cruise	5'7
Sylvester Stallone	5'7
Vin Diesel	6'1
Idris Elba	6'3
Dwayne Johnson	6'5

Since it is important in American culture for men to be tall to exert power, actors are made to look taller in their films. And that is why when Mark Walberg (5'8) shares a kiss with Charlize Theron (5'10) in *The Italian Job* they are sitting down.

Physiology

How you are physically influences your perceptions. Two examples:

- The world is made for average size people (no matter what that average is). People who are shorter than average or taller than average might perceive the world as uncomfortable.

© LStockStudio/Shutterstock.com

Look at the desk you are sitting in class. Is it comfortable? Do your feet touch the ground? Are your knees crunched up under the desktop?

- Your bio-rhythms: energized, fatigued, awake, sleepy, etc. will affect how you view the world. You need to understand these rhythms so you can choose the best for your college classes. If you are a night person, it's probably not a good idea to take early morning classes.

DANCING TO YOUR BIO-RHYTHMS

Design the best class schedule for you based on your bio-rhythms. You are a full-time student so you will need to schedule five classes.

Monday	Tuesday	Wednesday	Thursday	Friday

How would this schedule influence your perceptions of your classes?

Culture

The various cultures from which you come influence your perceptions. How you answer the following questions will explain to others why you think they don't do things correctly.

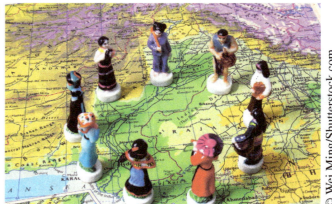

- What is the correct way to set a dinner table?
- In a household, who takes out the garbage?
- Can you put your feet on the furniture in your home?

Or we can look at wider culture and ask

- Can men and women touch in public?
- What is appropriate dress?
- What is the correct way to greet someone in the street?
- How close does one stand to a stranger when conversing in public?

Technology

Technological competence is important to us these days. Our perception of people, places, and things is influenced by the technology they use.

- A college is not "real" if it doesn't have smart classrooms.
- Old people are not smart because they can't or don't use computers.
- Your friend is strange because your friend has no cell phone.

© Wei Ming/Shutterstock.com

© Pumtek/Shutterstock.com

Halo or Horns Effect

Your perceptions are influenced by a person's characteristics.

© Art Konobalov/Shutterstock.com

- Halo Effect: You see one good characteristic in a person you are likely to see that person as generally good. You will explain away bad behavior so as to keep the good opinion you have of that person.
- Horns Effect: You see one negative characteristic in a person that person becomes entirely negative to you. Even that person's good deeds are given a sinister or self-serving motive.

Attribution

Attribution is our attempt to figure out why people do what they do so we know how to react to them.

In order to do this figuring out we ask two questions.

© Rawpixel.com/Shutterstock.com

- Who is responsible?
- Why did this happen?

As people we are prone to want to know why things happen. Our justice system is in some ways based on this want. It is very difficult to get a conviction unless the prosecution can establish a clear motive—a why—for the crime. Juries are uneasy about convicting someone without knowing why that person would have done the crime.

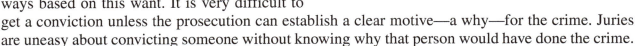

We look at the information given to us in any given communication situation to answer the "who" and "why" question. Sometimes we are right, sometimes we are wrong. Nevertheless, the answers to these questions affect our perceptions. Two examples:

- Who is responsible?
  - ❏ If we believe circumstances are out of a person's control, then we will view their behaviors more favorably even if those behaviors are negative.
- Why did this happen?
  - ❏ If we believe that people are in control or do have responsibility, then we perceive their behaviors negatively.

Here are two aspects of Attribution to watch out for:

- The Fundamental Attribution Error.
  - ❏ You base your judgments more on personal characteristics then on external circumstances when answering the "who and why" question. (McPherson and Young, 2004).

- Self-serving Bias:
  - ❏ I am responsible for an outcome when that outcome is positive. I blame others when that outcome is negative. I got an "A." My professor gave me a "D."
  - ❏ I put my own actions in a positive light and other's actions in a negative light. "I am righteous indignant in a good cause." "You are just angry." (Shephed et al., 2008)

Needs

You perceive what you want or need to perceive at any given time.

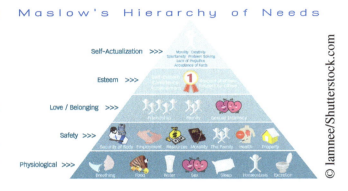

Maslow's Hierarchy of Needs

© Iamnee/Shutterstock.com

You are not seeing what is actually there, but what you want or need to be there.

We do this when we date people, interpreting that the person is interested because we need that as opposed to that person's just being polite.

We do this when we filter out messages that conflict with what we want for ourselves or what we think of ourselves. Confirmation bias plays a role here as well. You need to feel you are right so you attend to those things that support your position.

So Now What?

Perception Inventory

What do you know about perception now? You know that people view the world differently. Your understanding of the world is not another's understanding of the world. A person's message reflects that person's understanding and your response to that person's message reflects yours. Perceptions are communicated as best they can be in the hopes of exchanging meaning. How do you help meaning exchange along? Try this:

© billdayone/Shutterstock.com

- Assume differing perceptions.
  - ❏ Sender and receiver are different people who view the world differently
  - ❏ Sender and receiver are selectively attending to different stimuli
  - ❏ Sender and receiver are organizing stimuli differently, therefore
  - ❏ Sender and receiver interpret differently.

- Ask "what am I not seeing?"
- Put yourself in another's shoes. Try to view the world the way others' do.
  - ❏ You don't have to like the way others see the world.
  - ❏ Understanding how they do will help you be a better communicator.

Answers for quiz on p. 5.

✳ Dirty Harry

✳ Titanic

✳ Terminator

✳ Star Wars (take your pick)

✳ The Wizard of Oz

✳ The Shining

✳ Jaws

✳ The Princess Bride

✳ Toy Story

✳ Star Trek: The Wrath of Khan

Chapter 4

"I'm pretty sure there's a lot more to life than being really, really, ridiculously good looking. And I plan on finding out what that is."

—Derek Zoolander, *Zoolander*

A Discussion of Self-Concept

The starting point of all communication with others is the self.

- Our messages are made up of who we are—our beliefs, attitudes, values, behaviors, and experiences.
- Who we are affects every aspect of communication including:
  - ❏ the environment around us
  - ❏ our own behavior
  - ❏ the behavior of others
- The better you understand yourself and the better you feel about that self, the more effective your communication will be.
- You are likely to be unsuccessful in communicating with others if you have a poor opinion of yourself. You believe your communication will fail so it will.

© Alexander Image/Shutterstock.com

We have many different selves. Let's look at them with an eye toward improving our communication with ourselves and others.

SELF-IDENTITY

Your self-identity is who you believe yourself to be. This belief is based on your assessment of five aspects of who you are.

The Physical Self

Your assessment of who you are physically is what makes up the Physical Self. Aspects of the physical self includes:

- Height
- Weight
- Body shape
- Attractiveness
- Gender
- Human ability
- Intelligence
- Ethnicity

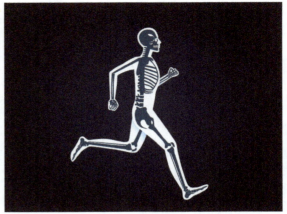

You assess these things and make judgments about them. Those judgments affect your sense of who you are. You may compare yourself to others using some of these characteristics or all of them. You, like Derek Zoolander, may feel that you are really, really, really ridiculously good looking, you may think you are just average, you may believe that you are unattractive or inferior to some degree. These assessments will influence your communication with yourself or others. Regarding the last assessment, you may see yourself one way while others see you in a more realistic way.

Social Self

Your social self is comprised of the roles you play in society at large.

We use our roles to communicate with others. The roles you play will dictate how you communicate.

The woman in the photograph serves her country in the military, and cares for and teaches her daughter. These responsibilities require different communication roles.

You play many roles every day. You might be

- A student
- An employee
- A sibling

- A spouse
- A mentor
- A volunteer
- A team member
- A pedestrian
- A driver

These roles help define the social relationships you have with others. They also indicate the type and amount of communication you will engage in. Your role as a parent is very different than your role as a student.

Psychological Self

This self includes your understanding of your personality, your emotional state, your needs, and of course, your beliefs, attitudes, and values.

You assess yourself and then label yourself as friendly, shy, sophisticated, caring, warm, energetic, and intelligent.

Beliefs, values, and attitudes are defined by labels such as:

- Radical or conservative or liberal
- Pro-life or pro-choice
- Religious or spiritual or nonreligious
- Meat eater or vegetarian or vegan

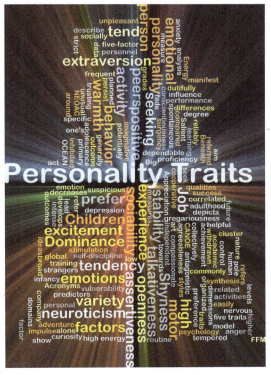

© Kheng Guan Toh/Shutterstock.com

Moral Self

You assess yourselves in terms of how well you live up to your core values. Values like being:

- Respectful
- Honest
- Fair
- Trustworthy
- Loyal
- Nonbiased

© kareInoppe/Shutterstock.com

Your core values may have been instilled in you by your parents, educators, culture, religion, or your own search for truth and what is right for you. Regardless of where you got them, they are the most important part of who you are.

You know this to be true because you know how you feel about yourself when you violate a moral principle you have chosen to live by. For example, a vegan will not eat or wear anything made from an animal product but sometimes may be tempted to have a grilled, nonvegan cheese sandwich. To stay true to your belief, you do not eat the sandwich if someone is looking or more importantly, if no one is looking.

Behavioral Self

Your behavioral self is what you do. You are a

- Basketball player
- Carpenter
- Cook
- Camper
- Pianist
- Painter
- Rapper
- Sports fan (choose your team)

Such behaviors give you a lot to talk about with others. They may influence your social roles.

We value some aspects of our self-identity over others.

- Our body shape and weight may be the most important aspect of our self-identity.
- Or, we may value our roles as students over our hobbies and interests.

Regardless of how much importance you put on, say your behavioral self (the first thing you tell others about yourself is that you are a fan of the football player Michael Vick), as a vegan or animal rights advocate, you would abandon that fandom when you learn he ran a dog fighting operation and abused animals because this conflicts with your moral self.

WHO AM I?

Using the categories from the previous page make an inventory of who you are.

Physical Self

Social Self

Psychological Self

Moral Self

Behavioral Self

BE YOURSELF
but be your best self

© Vasileios Karafillidis /Shutterstock.com

IDEAL SELF

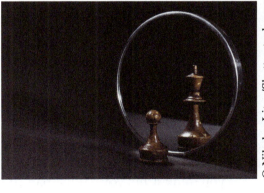

Your ideal self is the picture you have in your head of who you would be in a perfect world. The ideal self is something you strive to be. It may not be someone you are at the moment.

- The ideal self has the same five dimensions as the self-identity.
- For example, you may perceive yourself as not very funny, but have an ideal picture of yourself as a witty person.
- Your ideal self is often different than who you believe you have the potential to become.
  - Therefore, we sometimes have trouble liking ourselves.
  - We know what we should do and how we should behave, but we don't do it. We lose focus on the ideal self we strive to be.

The gap between who we are (self-identity) and who we want to be (ideal self) is where our self-esteem resides.

The closer your ideal self is to your self-identity the more likely it is that you will feel good about yourself and therefore communicate well.

Clearly, part of the equation here is the value you place on the characteristics that are far apart (big gap between the ideal self and self-identity). If the characteristic is important to you and there is a big gap between who you are and who you would like to be, you may be a less effective communicator and less successful overall.

SELF-IMAGE

Your self-image is how you define yourself. Self-image is how we look at ourselves in relation to our jobs, our career goals, our family, our relationships, our interests, etc. What is the first thing you tell someone about yourself when you are introduced? Is it your name? Is it what you do for a living? Is it your relationships? How you respond to people when you meet them for the first time reflects your image of yourself at that time.

Below are a few ways you may define yourself

© Everett Collection/Shutterstock.com

Names

Do you like your name? If you could change it what would you change it to? Why?

Do you think it fits you? What part of your self-identity is best represented by your name? How might your name influence how you view yourself?

Does your name reflect the ideal picture you have of yourself?

Does your name tie you to a famous or infamous family in your community? How did your name affect your life at school?

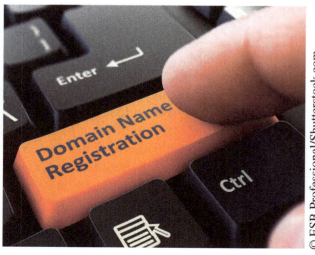

© ESB Professional/Shutterstock.com

Jobs

If you are currently employed do you like your job? Does your job speak to who you are or is a temporary thing you do to make money?

Some jobs are considered prestigious and others not. This is one of the reasons grandiose titles are applied to what society currently believes are low prestige jobs. Can you figure out what job you would have if you applied for the following?

- Sanitation Engineer _____
- Relationship Representative _____
- Business Communication Conveyor _____
- Office Hygiene Control Specialist _____
- Printed Document Handler _____

These titles are designed to make the jobs look more prestigious than they are. Such titles help people feel better about what they do for a living.

Roles

What roles do you use to define yourself?

- Student
- Parent
- Employee
- Athlete

You define yourself by different roles in different situations. At a parent or teacher conference you communicate as a parent. You would do so even if you yourself were a teacher.

Cultural background

Do you celebrate your cultural heritage? Do you define yourself as a member of a particular cultural group?

If you do identify with a culture what beliefs, attitudes, and values do you hold as a result. What behaviors do you engage in as a result?

The photograph is of two members of the Nez Perce nation—I-ah-to-tonah, or Little Woman Mountain, and her son A-last-Sauked, or Looking-away-off. The photo was taken in 1909. What do you learn about this mother and son from looking at this photograph?

Self-Identity

If you love music you may define yourself first and foremost as a musician or in the case of the gentlemen to the left, rappers.

You might choose the most important part of your self-identity and use that to introduce yourself to the world.

© AS photo studio/Shutterstock.com

Religion

You might define yourself by the faith you hold. You might define yourself as holding no faith.

The three women pictured on the left represent three different faiths. You know that because they have chosen to define themselves as part of a faith group by what they are wearing.

No matter how you self-identify, you are not unlike many of the people you interact and communicate with and you should not pass judgement on others who may be experiencing some of your same challenges or challenges and

© Mila Supinskaya Glashchenko /Shutterstock.com

difficulties of their own. As you watch this video think about yourself, how you identify and if you would be brave enough to share or Self-Disclose (we will explore this in the next section) the way these other students have.

MIRROR, MIRROR

SELF-IMAGE INVENTORY

Using the information above conduct a self-image inventory. What do you discover about yourself?

Name

Job

Roles

Culture

Self-Identity

Religion

SELF-ESTEEM

© Syda Productions /Shutterstock.com

Self-esteem is another way of talking about self-respect. You analyze who you are and decide on any given day or at any given time how much or little you respect yourself. You know that you can be pretty tough on yourself. Sometimes you like yourself and sometimes you don't. Sometimes you respect yourself and sometimes you don't. Sometimes you care what happens to you and sometimes you don't.

Your changing evaluation of yourself is influenced by what influences your perceptions:

- Past experience
- Emotions
- Attitudes
- Beliefs
- Culture
- Technology
- Physiology

The good news here is that your self-evaluation is not static. It can change. The changes are based on among other things

- Context
- Competency in how you play the roles you assume
- Adhering to your moral code

The point is that your evaluation of yourself can and does change. You are not stuck with a poor evaluation of yourself if you don't want to be.

SELF-DISCLOSURE

The key to building and maintaining relationships is self-disclosure. Self-disclosure is the act of telling someone something about yourself for the primary purpose of moving the relationship forward, maintaining the relationship where it is or ending the relationship.

The type and amount of self-disclosure you do in a relationship indicates to others the kind of relationship you wish to have with them. Not everyone understands this truth about self-disclosure, but now you do. You can now begin to make the choices you need to make to have better relationships.

A simple definition of self-disclosure is "telling someone something about yourself." But as with most things in communication studies self-disclosure involves more than that.

For self-disclosure to be genuine the following must be present:

- The information you share must be personal.
- The message must be primarily verbal.
- Another person must be involved.
- Those involved must disclose the same type and amount of information.

In other words, the message must be personal, must be sent to another person and must be sent with the express purpose of building, maintaining, or ending a relationship.

The information you share must be personal

That sounds easy. But of course, it is not. The biggest difficulty we face in engaging in effective self-disclosure is our differing understandings of "personal information."

We each have our own understanding of what constitutes personal information. You may be perfectly willing to tell someone your shoe size because you don't consider that personal information. Others do, for whatever reason, consider shoe size personal and will be unwilling to reveal that information to you.

There are many reasons why people make the "personal or not personal information" choice. We will look at those later. It is enough to know right now that no two people are alike in this respect.

WHAT DO WE MEAN BY PERSONAL?

Make a list of the types of things you think constitute personal information.

What makes these things personal to you?

How does your belief about what constitutes personal information influence your communication with others?

The message must be primarily verbal

Clearly some personal information may be communicated nonverbally. Generally, this information is not considered self-disclosure as it is not information whose purpose is to build and maintain relationships.

© Ollyy/Shutterstock.com

Take, for example, the wedding ring.

The wedding ring is a cultural artifact whose purpose is to alert others to one's status within the community.

Such information is purposeful—you wear a wedding ring to indicate you are married. It is not an artifact designed for an interpersonal encounter that builds and maintains relationships. It is a declaration to the world at large that you are in a marriage. And while the wedding ring is supposed to indicate that one is not available as a potential partner, the only way an individual person would know that is to ask, so we are back to verbal.

As a side note: the wedding ring is not the only way to indicate marriage. Cultures differ on this marker.

- In the Amish community, a beard indicates a married man.
- In the Hindu community, the wife wears a pendent necklace to indicate your married status.
- In Poland, the wedding ring is worn on the right hand.

If you are unfamiliar with the culture you can run into some interesting problems because the non-verbal cue for marital status is invisible to you. In this case, there is no self-disclosure going on.

Another person must be involved

Alas, you cannot self-disclose to your cat, dog, parrot, computer, or houseplant. You can talk to them if you wish, but that conversation will not fulfill the purpose of self-disclosure.

You signal to others what type of relationship you think you have and the type of relationship you would like to have by the type and amount of personal information you share. That is how you build, maintain, or end relationships. Your cat, dog, parrot, computer, or houseplant cannot respond in a meaningful way that does any of those three things.

Those involved are disclosing the same type and amount of information

This final aspect of self-disclosure is the safety valve of the process. You can self-disclose in any way you choose, but the safe bet is to have equal self-disclosure in a relationship.

When you wish to up the ante, move the relationship to the next level, you proffer a piece of information about yourself. Then you wait to see how the other person responds. If it is with the same type and amount of information, then you know that the person is interested in building the relationship. If it isn't then you know that person is not ready yet or may never be ready to move past where the relationship currently stands.

Keep in mind that people have different understandings of what constitutes personal information. The reason you may not be getting the response you want is because the other person or people involved don't see your information as personal. They don't realize you are looking to move the relationship forward.

WHY DO WE SELF-DISCLOSE?

The answer is to build, maintain, or end relationships. However, there are other factors to consider. It is important to consider these factors as they affect the success of your communication.

Catharsis

Catharsis is a Latin form of the Greek word meaning "purifying or cleansing." In is a concept that is used in a variety of disciplines.

In Psychology, catharsis means the "release of negative emotions."

In literature, catharsis refers to a character's outpouring of emotion for cleansing purposes.

What these examples have in common is the idea of emotional release, of getting something off your chest. And so it is in self-concept. Catharsis is a compulsion to tell someone something. You have to do it or you'll burst.

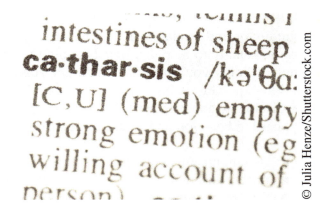

© Julia Henze/Shutterstock.com

- Positive aspects of catharsis include:
    - ❏ a feeling of relief
    - ❏ becoming more authentic to others
    - ❏ becoming more authentic to oneself
- Negative aspects of catharsis include:
    - ❏ revealing too much information
    - ❏ lack of self-monitoring
    - ❏ emotion over reason

Sharing

Another reason we self-disclose is we hope others will. We share something about ourselves and others reciprocate. We share

© Syda Productions/Shutterstock.com

- As a conversation starter:
    - ❏ On the line at the grocery store, we chat about low-risk personal information to pass the time.
    - ❏ At a party, we tell people what we do or some other low-risk information.
- To empathize or sympathize with others:
    - ❏ We share stories of loss with people who have just experienced a death.
    - ❏ We share embarrassing experiences to let people know that kind of thing can happen anyone.
- To set parameters for interpersonal communication:
    - ❏ You let people know you have just suffered a loss in the hope that no one will joke about death.
    - ❏ You let others know you have recently lost your job in the hopes that people will not talk about their great careers.

Self-Clarification

While self-disclosure is generally used to build, maintain, or end a relationship, it can also be used intra-personally to help you understanding yourself better. It helps you build and maintain your self-relationship. This is how self-clarification works. You disclose to another, using that person as a sounding board to help you understand yourself:

■ You are unsure about taking a new job.
■ You are unsure whether to stay in a relationship.
■ You are unsure of how you feel about an issue.

© Happy Stock Photo/Shutterstock.com

In all these instances, you talk with another. Verbalizing your confusion and asking for a response can help you figure out what you want to do.

Self-Validation

You might at some time have done something that embarrasses you or makes you feel uneasy. What do you do? You go to a sympathetic friend and tell the story. You expect that friend to agree that you did just the right thing. That is self-validation.

We like to know that how we think, what we believe and do is okay. We tell people what we think, believe and do in the hope that they will agree that we are right. When we engage in self-validation we are

© Rido/Shutterstock.com

■ careful in our choice of listener
■ not necessarily concerned with the truth
■ looking to assuage a negative emotion

Impression Enhancement

American etiquette rules state that the only people who can be introduced as "Dr." in a nonprofessional or social setting are people who hold medical degrees.

In a social setting people holding any other type of doctorate are not referred to by that title. Bummer for those who worked hard for the Ph.D.'s, Ed.'s, JD's, DFA's, DMA's and all the rest.

For those who wish others to know that they hold doctorates Impression Enhancement is the tool they use.

© Malchev/Shutterstock.com

- At a party: "What do you do for a living?" "Oh, my Ph.D. is in Antediluvian Structural Analysis so I spend my days cataloging my family's library. What do you do?"

American culture doesn't allow for boasting although it is fine with being proud of who you are and what you do. It pays to be careful about doing this kind of self-disclosure.

WHAT INFLUENCES SELF-DISCLOSURE?

Obviously self-disclosure does not take place in a vacuum. There are various influences on you and the other people in the relationship that encourages or discourages you to self-disclose. Here they are discussed.

© Alfa Photo/Shutterstock.com

Personality

Your personality type influences how and why you self-disclose.

- Some people are promiscuous self-disclosers. They have no filters and will self-disclose to anyone at any time. Sadly, you meet these people while standing on line.
- Then there are people who see much of the world as friendly. These people are open to self-disclosure but with some filters.
- Insecure people may self-disclose to get people to like them.
- Private people tend to be cautious self-disclosers.

© Keith Bell/Shutterstock.com

Competency

The more competent you are at making communication choices the more effective your self-disclosure will be.

- You can assess the communication situation to maximize meaning.
- You know what is appropriate to disclose and what is not.
- You can accurately interpret another's verbal and nonverbal cues.

© donskarpo/Shutterstock.com

Liking

This influence may seem obvious, but nothing about good communication is obvious.

<mark>We form bonds with people.</mark>

© elwynn/Shutterstock.com

- The tighter the bond, the more we like and trust a person the more likely self-disclosure will take place with that person.
- On the other hand, we can form instant intimacy which also encourages self-disclosure. Bartenders, strangers on a train or airplane are examples of people you might disclose to even though you barely have a relationship with these people.

Group Size

Most self-disclosure takes place in one-on-one situations or in small groups. We are talking here about conversations over coffee or self-help groups. There is safety in small numbers when self-disclosing.

You would think people who go on talk shows to air their dirty laundry would know this, but you would be wrong.

© Pensiri/Shutterstock.com

Topics

You will self-disclose based on the topics being discussed. When assessing this influence think about the following:

- If the topic discussed shows our strengths, we might self-disclose.
- If the topic shows our weaknesses, we may not.
- If the topic is too personal for the context and/or people involved, then no self-disclosure. Topics such as
  - ❏ Age
  - ❏ Employment

© Lightspring/Shutterstock.com

❏ Salary
❏ Education

can be no-go zones for parties or coffee shops where others can overhear the conversation.

Dyadic Effect

This is a powerful influence on self-disclosure as well as being a dangerous one.

The dyadic effect can be defined as *a compulsion to self-disclose because you were self-disclosed to.*

In other words, someone divulges some personal information to you and you feel compelled to divulge the same type and amount of information back.

Some suggestions for navigating the dyadic effect:

- Be empathic or sympathetic
    ❏ Mutual self-disclosure can be a good thing.
    ❏ Certainly, mutual self-disclosure can help in maintaining equity relationships.
- Danger Will Robinson!
    ❏ The person divulging this information may not consider it important where as you do. You are not communicating the same type and amount of information.
    ❏ Some people will divulge because they want certain information from you to use later and not in a friendly way.

Culture

Obviously, cultures differ as to the type and amount of self-disclosure appropriate across a range of relationships. Here are some examples:

- Americans are promiscuous self-disclosers.
- Japanese and Germans are reticent self-disclosers.

SELF-DISCLOSURE IS RISKY BUSINESS

It goes without saying, but we will say it anyway, that self-disclosure can be risky. Any time you offer someone a piece of personal information about yourself you open yourself up to being betrayed by that person's inability to keep things private.

© PHOTOCREO Michal Bednarek /Shutterstock.com

Ben Franklin's quote "three may keep a secret if two are dead" nicely sums up how to keep from getting hurt by revealing information about yourself to another. How can you minimize the risk of self-disclosure? Let's try this:

Make an inventory of what topics you consider to be low, medium, high, or not-telling-ever risk self-disclosure. For the list below put an "L", "M", "H", or "NTE" in the boxes next to the topic. We will discuss this in a moment.

	Acquaintance	Friend	Best Friend	Sibling	Parent	Significant Other
Age						
Height and weight						
Shoe size						
Music choices						
Take home pay						
What you pay for things						
Religion						
Place of origin						
Food likes and dislikes						
Politics						
Groups you belong to						
Sexual activities						
Sexual history						

Notice that your level of comfort in revealing information about yourself is directly influenced by

- How trustworthy you think your listener is.
- Who is entitled to the information.
- Why you need to self-disclose.
- What you consider to be personal information.

You reduce the risk of self-disclosure by making good choices, that is, answering the above how, who, why, what questions accurately.

You would not engage in self-disclosure if it was an all risk no rewards endeavor. Done well, self-disclosure has the following benefits:

© iQoncept/Shutterstock.com

Self-Knowledge

You learn more about yourself the more you self-disclose. Earlier we talked about self-clarification and self-validations as reasons why we self-disclose. Both reasons for self-disclosure help you learn about yourself.

© pathdoc/Shutterstock.com

Coping Abilities

Self-disclosure helps you learn to deal with your problems. The catharsis, self-clarification, and self-validation reasons for self-disclosing all help you figure out how to navigate the world.

Remember the dyadic effect? Others will self-disclose the same type and amount of information. Suddenly you realize that you are not alone. Others have had the same or similar problems.

© WindNight/Shutterstock.com

Communication Efficiency

Good self-disclosure promotes trust and honesty in relationships. The more you know of a person the better you can understand that person's communication.

The more you trust someone with information about yourself the more likely you are to be clear and truthful in your communication.

Relational Depth

The type and amount of self-disclosure you do indicates to another what kind of relationship you think you are in with that person.

Relationships become deep and personal when all the people in the relationship are disclosing personal information. You are not in relationship with someone if you are not disclosing to that person.

© William Perugini/Shutterstock.com

THE RISKS OF SELF-DISCLOSURE

Self-disclosure has a number of risks associated with it. After all you are telling people about yourself and there is nothing preventing that person from using that information against you. You leave yourself very vulnerable when you disclose. Here are some of the dangers.

© Svetlana Lukienko/Shutterstock.com

Rejection

The person you disclose to may not be able to accept what you have said. You may have encountered this in your own life when you told a person something you thought would help the relationship along, but it had the opposite effect.

This risk is often a catalyst in movies and books. The conflict, plot, or action is moved along because the self-disclosure causes a change in behavior.

In any great movie, there comes a point that Blake Snyder in his book *Save the Cat*, calls "the dark night of the soul." You can call this "the major setback" if you wish. It is at this point in a movie that the main characters have an argument and information is revealed that changes their relationships.

Usually the revelation—the self-disclosure—causes the best friend, love interest or team, to desert the hero. The rejection caused by this self-disclosure in the conflict that heightens the tension as the climax of the movie approaches. (http://www.storymastery.com/story/screenplay-structure-five-key-turning-points-successful-scripts/)

Material Loss

Self-disclosing can cause you to lose a job, a house, money, and a career.

Politicians face these issues when they are forced to admit to less than ethical behavior.

Mel Gibson lost his Hollywood career by disclosing his opinions to police officers. He is currently making a comeback, but that is not always possible.

MINIMIZING RISK

You might look at the above list and think, well I am not going to be self-disclosing any time soon. Sure, there are risks involved with self-disclosure, but there are ways to minimize the risk. Here are some guidelines for good self-disclosure.

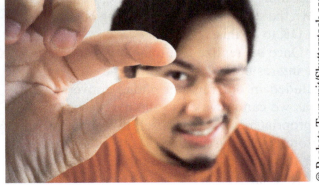

Acceptable risk is the goal

Don't go blurting out information to just anyone. Be mindful of the relationship and what the other can hear and deal with.

Ask yourself why you need to disclose this particular piece of information at this particular time. What do you hope to achieve by the self-disclosure?

By the way, this is why we self-disclose to bartenders and strangers on a train, bus, or airplane. We believe we will never see them again or that in the case of the bartender there is a code that prevents the bartender from revealing that information. We deem this acceptable risk.

© hafakot/Shutterstock.com

TMI

Don't dump all your deepest, darkest secrets on someone the first time you meet. Information you share is a gift you give someone. Start with small gifts and move to bigger ones until you think you have given enough. Disclosure grows with the relationship.

© Checubus/Shutterstock.com

There are times and places and people

We have a big problem today with people self-disclosing in public. They are on their phones, chatting away about the most personal things while standing on line, walking down the street, shopping, or dining out. It's not OK to do this.

Once we realize that total strangers are not interested and have no business being included in our random phone conversations we can move on to the next issue of appropriateness. Ask yourself this question before disclosing anything: Is this the person to whom I should be disclosing this information?

© Tomislav Zidanic/Shutterstock.com

Motive

You minimize risk by being honest with yourself about your motives. Why am I disclosing, you should be asking before you blurt out something.

If your answer is not to "strengthen my relationship and learn more about myself then perhaps you should not say anything."

© Michelle Patrick/Shutterstock.com

The feeling is mutual

Is this person disclosing the same type and amount of information you are? If not, what does that say and what should I do?

If you believe that the self-disclosure is not mutual, that there may be ulterior motives on the part of the other person, then you should be very careful about disclosing.

© Lightspring/Shutterstock.com

Will there be Problems?

Will the disclosure cause problems? Will you be burdened by the disclosure? Will the recipient be burdened?

It is not necessary nor is it wise to disclose everything to one person. There are some things others simply do not need to know about us.

© carballo/Shutterstock.com

SO HOW DID I GET HERE?

Up to this point we have looked at the various selves that make up each one of us. Now is the time to ask how we came into possession of all these selves. What influences our self-development? There are a number of things that influence us. Let's start with a look at Family labels and go on from there.

© GiroScience/Shutterstock.com

FAMILY LABELS

Families have ways of developing their own identities. Then they label themselves and the family members to re-inforce those identities. Here are a few examples of how families label.

© Monkey Business Images /Shutterstock.com

Race and Ethnicity

How does the family define this characteristic? How does the family exhibit to itself and the world its connection to race and ethnicity?

How does the family pass this understanding to the next generation?

- Family stories or legends
- Family names

© Andrey-Popov/Shutterstock.com

Behavior

Your family explains verbally and nonverbally what behaviors are valued, what behaviors elicit praise, and what behaviors are prohibited or frowned upon. Your choice is to abide by these strictures or to strike out on your own.

© Jaromir Chalabala/Shutterstock.com

Description or Labeling

Family members describe the roles we play in the family unit. You may also play these roles outside the family.

You may decide that you are funny because your parents continually label your behavior as funny.

You may try to live up to the label of athlete, the pretty one, the responsible one, even if you don't see yourself this way.

© Apple Art/Shutterstock.com

Religion

Families describe who they are based on the belief system they adhere to.

Do you still hold the beliefs of your family? Have you moved away from them? If you have moved away do those beliefs still affect your worldview?

You may recognize the horse and buggy in the photograph. This is a typical Amish mode of transportation.

The Amish are a religious folk living in Pennsylvania, New York, Ohio, and Indiana although they are also found in other places in the United States. Their religious beliefs

© jimwolf photos/Shutterstock.com

require that they separate themselves from the world, abstain from the use of modern conveniences, dress in a plain fashion and practice humility. Failure to adhere to the strictures of the faith can result in excommunication, removal from the community.

GEOGRAPHY

Who you are, how you understand yourself, and how you are described are influenced by where you come from. This description can range from very specific—we are from Tipperary Hill; to less specific—we are from Syracuse; to general—we are from New York State.

It can be "we are Americans." It can be "we are rural" or "we are urban."

Since people are stereotyped by geography if

- You are from the South you must be stupid.
- You are from the city you must be a gangster.
- You are from Japan you must be smart.

This label can have a profound impact on you.

© Rainer Lesniewski/Shutterstock.com

CULTURE

This influence is different from race and ethnicity. You are described through your culture and your family acknowledge.

- Language
- Food
- Dress
- Artifacts

Included in this influence is how family is defined, what is expected of you, and who you are supposed to marry.

RULES

In this context, rules refer to the guidelines for living and guidelines for how you understand your identity.

Remember those scripts we talked about in the chapter on perception? Scripts are rules that your family and the culture set down that indicate what is acceptable and unacceptable behavior, ways of thinking, and ways of being. Here are some examples:

- Family:
  - ❏ "You are the oldest, so have to be responsible."
  - ❏ "We are hardworking people."

© ESB Professional/Shutterstock.com

© Annasunny24/Shutterstock.com

❏ "Save your money."
❏ "We don't marry outside our group."

These roles and attitudes are formed very early in life. Parents impress them on children as a way for children to deal with life.

MEDIA AND TECHNOLOGY

Media and technology set standards that then influence us. We might measure ourselves against these standards, drawing conclusions that affect our sense of self. Media include radio, TV, movies, magazines, newspapers, music, and the Internet. Some examples of media influence are the following.

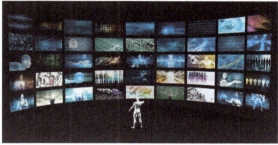
© kentoh/Shutterstock.com

Standards of Living

Poor people in TV shows don't really look poor. Of course, try finding a show in which the main characters are poor. Many TV shows depict lifestyles most of us will never achieve.

Don't you ever wonder how people who don't appear to work can afford those New York apartments?

We know why so many Marvel and DC super heroes are wealthy. They can buy all those fun gadgets and they have plenty of time on their hands.

Because it looks like everyone has a rich and

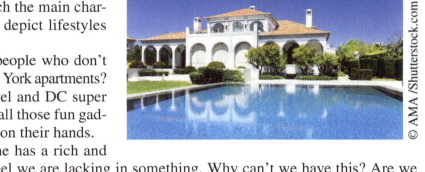
© AMA /Shutterstock.com

satisfying life we may begin to feel we are lacking in something. Why can't we have this? Are we bad providers for our families? Are we never going to be successful?

Perfection

Media portray people at the height of their abilities. How do we match up?

Could we really drive a car on two wheels?
Be as physically brave as movie heroes?
Never seem to need sleep?
Always connect the dots at the right time and solve the problem or save those in danger?
You may not be able to, but people in movies, on TV, and in your videogames always seem to be able to do these things.

© Bplanet/Shutterstock.com

Standards of Attractiveness

The media portrays images of what is currently considered attractive and that influences how we view ourselves. Remember that these views of attractiveness change over time. That keeps you in a constant whirl of stress if you believe you need to present as this perfect person.

We use referent power to copy the latest star.

We choose hair styles, make up, clothes, ways of walking, and speaking to copy what the Media tell us is fashionable or cool.

If we don't measure up, we do odd things like diet, workout excessively, and find ourselves way too interested in who we look and not who we are.

Standards of Competence

How well do we navigate the new cyber-world?

Your sense of who you are and how competent you are is affected by how comfortable you feel in the cyber world.

Adults often feel incompetent next to their children when it comes to computers. Who then has the authority and power?

In your favorite movies, you see computer geniuses saving the day, hacking into unhackable computers, and designing unbeatable cyber-weapons.

The perfection found in media depictions of life will affect how you understand yourself. How do you respond?

REFLECTED APPRAISAL

I know what you're thinking: I don't care what other people say about me. Sure. But we can't get very far in successful communication, if we are unwilling to entertain others' thoughts about us. It's actually a good idea. You can gain valuable insight into who you are. But do be careful. Test what you hear. Choose a few close friends to listen to and don't take freelance advice from anyone who cares to give it. Keep what you want, reject what you don't.

People who constantly say negative and discouraging things to you that no one else is saying are creating a toxic relationship and environment that you do not need to tolerate, especially if they are denigrating you to the point where your self-esteem is lowered or damaged. Sometimes this happens with people we are close to such as family or your significant other and even though it can be very difficult, end the relationship. Keep in mind they, not you, are the one with the problem.

Listening to others to understand ourselves better is called reflected appraisal. Think of it as using others as a mirror.

This mirror helps us navigate the world around us. You need to decide if you are going to conform to social norms or not. If you decide you will then look at the people around you who will tell you which behaviors are acceptable and which are not. This is how we learn to interact in social situations.

SOCIAL COMPARISON

We form an understanding of ourselves by how we measure up to those around us. We use other people for all sorts of measures. Usually we do this to help us know if we are making progress in the world. We use others to help us judge our abilities, talents, character, etc.

We compare ourselves to others in two ways:

- Alike or Different. How alike or different are we from others? This allows us to decide where we fit and where we want to fit. Example: background, gender, schooling, and beliefs.
- Relation to Others. Where am I in relation to others? Am I as smart, accomplished, successful? Now, how do I feel about the comparison? Is it a valid comparison?

Think about it: The High School Reunion

Have you or someone you know been to a High School reunion? _____
What did you or this person say about it? _____.
What might be a typical response? _____.
Tell a High School Reunion story. _____.

HOW SOCIETY OR CULTURE VIEWS THE WORLD

Each society, each culture is different. Norms of behavior, attitudes, dress, and values are part of what makes up a culture and explain why each culture and society is different. How you navigate through these norms affects your sense of self.

Cultures reveal their norms in two ways:

- Interactions with others. We learn all sorts of things: gender roles, class distinctions, modes of behavior, and the importance of the individual as we interact with others
- Media and institutions. These reflect cultural values. We have already talked about the media. Social institutions like marriage, our judicial system, and schools show what we value.

Your question is "how much or how little do I want to conform to the norms I see around me?"

SELF-FULFILLING PROPHESY

The self-fulfilling prophesy is a prediction or expectation you make or have about yourself that your behavior makes come true.

There are two possible ways to look at the self-fulfilling prophesy. The metaphor is based on the Greek myth of Pygmalion. The story goes that Pygmalion sculpted a statue and through a series of events with which I won't bore you he made the statue come alive. The myth was popular and was the basis of several stories and plays including the musical "My Fair Lady."

While the original story does not necessarily carry the connotation that Pygmalion "invented" the woman of his dreams and therefore has control over her, the later stories do suggest this. And so, we get to the following effects:

- Pygmalion Effect: We fulfill the expectations of others.
  - ❏ In the movie "Dead Poets Society" a student finally takes his own life because of the expectations of his family. They wanted him to be a doctor. That's not what he wanted to be.
  - ❏ Your parents expect you to go to their alma mater. You work hard in High School so you have the grade to get accepted to that college.
- The Galatea Effect: we fulfill our own expectations.
  - ❏ You expect to take over the family business so you learn the business.
  - ❏ You expect to pass a test so you study hard and you do.

THE IMPORTANCE OF THE "I"

Cultures differ in how they view the importance of the individual. This means that you derive part of your sense of who you are based on your adherence to the cultural norm. Do you evaluate yourself positively because you are a unique individual? Or do you have a positive evaluation because you are an outstanding member of your group or clan?

The scale runs for highly individualistic cultures to highly collectivist cultures.

- Individualistic cultures (North America/Western Europe) can be characterized by the following:
  - ❏ Idiocentric. The prime actor at the center of the culture is the individual.
  - ❏ Personal achievement is expected and rewarded.
  - ❏ Self is the first priority. The good of the one outweighs the good of the many.
  - ❏ Nonconformity is tolerated and can be celebrated.
  - ❏ Individual rights are acknowledged and enforced.
  - ❏ Language that reflects the primacy of the individual.

- Collectivist (Asia, Africa, Central/South America):
    - ❏ Allocentric. The primary actor at the center of the culture is the group:
        - Family
        - Tribe
        - Village
    - ❏ Group cohesion is of primary importance.
    - ❏ Conformity is important.
    - ❏ Nonconformity is suppressed.
    - ❏ Group goals outweigh individual concerns.
    - ❏ The good of the many outweigh the good of the one.
    - ❏ Language reflects the primacy of the group.

You can see how these cultural dynamics effect your understanding of who you are.

CULTURE CLASH

Choose two cultures in which you live, one individualistic and one collectivist. In the columns below list a few characteristics of those cultures. Be prepared to discuss them.

Individualistic	Collectivist

IDENTITY MANAGEMENT

Identity management is the key to good communication. Why is that? Because every day you make choices about how you are going to present yourself both in your private life and your public life. The better you are at making the right choices the more effective your communication will be.

You have two selves. Actually, you have many selves, but two primary ones:

- Private Self—sometimes called the "perceived self." This self is how you behave at home or when you think no one is watching.
- Public Self—sometimes called the "presenting self." This is what you let the world see of you.

The difference between the two can be summed up by your answer to the question "Do you play air guitar in your car when you know someone is watching?"

Private or Perceived Self: Behaviors, beliefs, and attitudes that we keep private

You look at yourself and see certain things.

- Your self-identity
- Your beliefs
- Your attitudes
- Your values
- Your behaviors

If you are honest with yourself, you will make an honest appraisal of these things.

You will probably not share most of this knowledge with others.

If you like what you have learned, you might take some of it out into the world with you. If you don't like it, you probably won't.

- Example: Habits
    - Cracking knuckles.
    - Humming tunelessly.
    - Repeating the same nonsense words over and over again.

- Example: Dress
    - We have clothing we wear in the house, but not in public.
    - We have indoor shoes and outdoor shoes.
    - We wear message tee-shirts in the house that would get us physically assaulted if we wore them in public.

- Example: Grief
    - We try to keep our grief private.
    - We cry in private and hope not to do that in public.
    - We find doing the littlest things difficult and so don't make the effort in private, but try to make an effort in public.

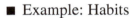

© Eric Issele/Shutterstock.com

Public or Presenting Self: How you decide to present yourself in public

These are roles we create and play in public to make communication work and help us to be happy and well-liked in the wider world.

Or these are roles we choose so we can stand athwart society and say, "I am unique."

You have by this time in your life decided how you wish to be seen by others. Not that this decision is static. You may decide to change it at any time, but the point is you **have** made a decision and are carrying it out.

To be an effective communicator you need to make conscience decisions about how you will present yourself to the world around you.

© Nejron Photo/Shutterstock.com

- If you are not making these conscience decisions already, start now.
- The less control you exercise over your public self, the less likely it is that you will be successful in life.

What does it mean to manage your impression? It means being aware of as many aspects of yourself and the world around you as possible.

- It means looking at the self-identity and deciding how to best highlight all five areas of that identity.
- It means taking special care to understand the roles you will be playing during the day and how best to play them.
- It means being aware of where you are going and the norms expected in that venue.
- It means knowing who you are likely to encounter and preparing for that.

Successful impression management requires you to be a high self-monitored person:

- High self-monitors are very aware of their public selves and work to make them as effective as possible.
- These people can handle social situations smoothly.
- They are good at reading people and therefore responding appropriately.
- These people have a broad range of behaviors and use them.

Less successful impression managers are low self-monitored people:

- Low self-monitoring people are not aware of their public selves.
- They have a simple, narrow focus of who they are.
- They have a smaller range of behaviors.
- Those behaviors are likely to be ineffective in many communication situations.
- They are less effective in their communication because they are not good at reading people.

IMPRESSION MANAGEMENT EXERCISE

Make a list of everything you did today to prepare for coming to class as a student:

Now choose a second role you have played or will play today and make a list of all the things you did to prepare to play that role.

Compare your lists. What is the same? What is different?

How effective was your communication in each role?

DEVELOPING AN ACADEMIC AND PROFESSIONAL "BRAND" AS PART OF OUR PUBLIC OR PRESENTING SELF

© marekuliasz/Shutterstock.com

Academic and professional "brands" are important to develop and to protect at all costs. What is a "brand?" It is the way products are identified by the public.

- A big yellow "M"
- A blue square with a lowercase white "f"
- A cartoon white ghost on a bright yellow square
- A fat bottomed checkmark
- A profile picture of an apple with a bite out of it

You know what these are. Nothing else needs to be said.

Now let's look at our "brand" or how we represent our product, which is ourselves. Our logo is our appearance including:

- What we wear?
- How we smell?
- How our hair looks?
- If our shoes our presentable?

All of this is part of our image. This is especially important when interviewing at a college or for a job. In no scenario is the expression "dress for success" more applicable. Men should dress, in most cases, business casual and a tie never hurts. Women should dress conservatively, and not wear short skirts, tight clothes, or low-cut blouses. Neutral colors are best and keep the jewelry, makeup, and perfume to a minimum.

Do not wear to an interview

Interview

Wear to an interview

The rest of the offering includes our characteristics, skills, experience, education, volunteer work such as Service Learning and the ability to speak about ourselves confidently.

Let's look closely at ourselves and work on creating our "brand."

Write 10 words that describe you (share these with the class) *

1)
2)
3)
4)
5)
6)
7)
8)
9)
10)

The Resume

As a part of building our brands, we will need to have a good resume to capture our public self. Since our public self is different than our private self there are some do's and don'ts for resumes. Do be professional. Don't be cutesy. White or ecru paper, a readable font Ariel as opposed to Comic Sans, and standard spacing and margins are essential.

The parts of the resume include:

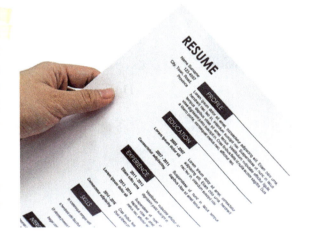

- Heading (name, address, cell phone number, and email address). Make sure email address is your name:
  - ❏ p.johnston@gmail.com—YES;
  - ❏ sweetkisser90@yahoo.com—NO!

Always make sure to answer your cell phone professionally and that you have a professional voicemail message for when you are unavailable.

- Summary (a statement about your characteristics and attributes).
- Skills (specific to what you know such as Microsoft programs, sales, cashiering, writing, speaking, tutoring, mentoring, waiting tables) and these skills should be evident in the experience section.
- Experience (work history in order of the last job first and should include month and year of employment, company name, your title, and a bullet list of responsibilities in past tense if not working there anymore or present tense if working there currently).
- Education (high school is fine if you are a recent grad, GED and date of completion, expected graduation date from present school and major).
- Volunteer work (it is a really good idea to do some sort of community or Service Learning).

Employers no longer want to see:

- An "objective," which is a statement that speaks to what you are looking for in a job. They are looking specifically for what you can bring to the company as an employee—what you can do for them; not what they can do for you.
- "References Available Upon Request."
- A list of personal interests.

Employers have many resumes to review and little time to review them so the information should be well organized, clear, concise, and customized for each new opportunity. You will find a sample resume at the end of the chapter.

You now know how to create your image by dressing to impress when meeting with college and workforce professionals. Once you have your resume which describes your characteristics, skills, work and volunteer experiences, and education; you are now well underway to developing your amazing "brand!"

The Interview

What is critical now is to practice interviewing to become confident in presenting yourself as an excellent potential transfer student or employee. Colleges and companies are looking for candidates who can competently communicate their strengths and enthusiasm.

© tsyhun/Shutterstock.com

Before the interview you should research the school or company. You do this

- To demonstrate your interest specifically in that organization.
- To understand why you are a good fit for them and they are a good fit for you.

For an interview remember the saying is, if you are early—you are on time; if you are on time—you are late; if you are late—don't bother.

Also for a successful interview:

- Leave your cell phone in your car or turned off (not vibrate) in your pocket or bag.
- Bring an extra copy of your resume, a note book, and pen.
- Prepare 2–3 questions about the job or organization to ask at the interview. The question should be something like, "What does a successful employee look like to you?" or "What do you like most about this college or working for this company?" Do not ask a question like, "How soon can I get a raise?"
- Use a firm handshake, good eye contact, smile, spit out the gum, and thank the interviewer for their time.
- Send a thank you note or email (get the person's contact information).
- Prepare what you will say, plan what you will wear, and how you will get to the interview, and practice, practice, practice.

Beware of the Social Media Meltdown

So now through self-discovery and disclosure you have developed your "brand." Now you must protect it.

© Rawpixel.com/Shutterstock.com

This means, if you are serious about advancing toward your ideal self, you will be very careful about everything you put on social media. You will need to clean up your Facebook, Instagram, Snapchat, and all other accounts.

Schools and employers WILL find you on social media and if you are not very careful about what you post about yourself, who you follow and what others send you, then you can completely damage your image and your "brand" and lose out on academic and professional opportunities. Be smart, it is never good to post pictures of yourself at a wild party or doing illegal things, saying negative things about school, work or coworkers, or to use profanity.

SAMPLE RESUME

<table>
<tr>
<td colspan="2" align="center">

Robby Z. Woods

103 Isabell Rd, Apt. B, Syracuse, N.Y. 13210

(315-000-0000) Robby.Woods@email.com

</td>
</tr>
<tr>
<td>Summary</td>
<td>I am driven and passionate with a strong desire to succeed in healthcare. As an Army combat veteran I am disciplined, detail oriented, organized with the ability to remain composed under stress while following directions and protocol. I am compassionate, patient, and enjoy working with diverse groups of people. I am a strong team member with the competence to work independently. I understand the importance of demonstrating empathy, flexibility, and staying current on new technologies, treatments, and regulations.</td>
</tr>
<tr>
<td>Skills</td>
<td>

• Customer Service

• Leadership

• Food Service Safety

• Coaching

• Time Management

• Secret Security Clearance

• Microsoft Programs

  -Word

  -Excel

  -PowerPoint

</td>
</tr>
</table>

Experience 3/16–5/16	**Gill Grilling Company, Syracuse, NY** Assistant Chef (Seasonal) • Managed kitchen • Provided excellent customer service • Cater to individual diets • Follow "ServSafe" protocol
9/15–3/16	**Embassy Suites, East Syracuse, NY** Line Cook • Provided excellent customer service • Cater to individual diets • Follow "ServSafe" protocol
5/12–9/15	**U.S. Army, Fort Drum, NY** Soldier/ Infantryman • Team Leader • Weapon Specialist • Counter-IED Specialist
01/11–01/12	**Holiday Inn, Liverpool, NY** Line Cook • Provided excellent customer service • Catered to individual diets • Followed "ServSafe" protocol
Volunteer **Summer** **2016**	**NYSWYSA, Syracuse, NY** *Youth Soccer Coach* • Taught soccer fundamentals • Promoted team cohesion • Maintained safety of youth
Education 2015–2017 09/05/2016	• A.A. in Humanities, Onondaga Community College, Syracuse, NY • First Aid/CPR Certification

Answers to the Jobs question (pg. 7)
Garbage collector
Bank teller
Courier
Janitor
Typist

Chapter 5

"I don't think that word means what you think it means"

—Inigo Montoya, *The Princess Bride*

A Discussion of Verbal Communication

© exopixel/Shutterstock.com

Verbal Communication is defined as "the words we use." That's it. Everything else, including *how* we say words, what is sometimes called paralanguage or vocalics, is considered nonverbal. Don't think that just because language is such a small percentage of our overall communication arsenal that it is unimportant. We don't have proverbs like "Sticks and stones may break my bones but names will never harm me" because we think it's true. We know that words are important. So, let's jump right in and discuss verbal communication.

WHAT DOES THIS MEAN?

Define the following terms:
I am folically challenged.

Eschew Obfuscation.

Ghoughteighpteau.

It takes some time to figure out what this language use actually means. Knowing that, you can understand how difficult it is to exchange meaning verbally.

- The first phrase is a euphemism. This phrase is purposefully designed to hide its meaning—which is "I am bald."
- The second example illustrates that there are many words in the English language, some of them are multi-syllabic, and you can't be expected to know all of them. (The phrase means "don't be obscure.")
- The third instance is brought to us by Bingham (2007) and illustrates the difficulty of English spelling. That word is "potato."

SPELLING FUN

Take a stab at it. Make up three different spellings of your name. If your name is MacKensie you are in luck. There are 45 recognized spellings of this name.

1)

2)

3)

Later on, we will discuss why having so many spelling options is a problem.

As a literate as opposed to a pre-literate society—meaning that we have a written language—Americans have two ways of communicating through language. We write and we speak.

Not all peoples have a written language. Of the approximately 7000 languages currently spoken in the world, about half of them have no written language (Simon and Fenning, 2017). These cultures do not encounter the spelling issue illustrated by the many ways one could spell "potato" in English or the many ways you can spell your name. That does not mean it is easier for pre-literate cultures to communicate verbally. All languages have common characteristics that make meaning exchange difficult.

THERE ARE RULES

The particular language(s) that you speak, read, and/or write have rules. These rules are universally accepted by the speakers of the language and form the basis by which people understand one another.

Those rules include the following.

Syntax

The arrangement of words, phrasing, and punctuation is a good way to define syntax. American English is an SVO language. Usually sentences in English are subject, verb object. This is a fairly rigid system but can be altered if you wish.

Standard English: I ran down the street.
Still OK usage: Down the street I ran.
Yoda usage (still OK): The street I ran down.
Not OK: Ran the street I down.

Grammar

Grammar rules explain how words are used or can refer to the whole system and structure of a language.

Our old friends *their, there,* and *they're* must be used correctly or you are going to find meaning exchange Here are three examples:

Your, yore, and *you're* must be used correctly or meaning is not going to be exchanged.

To, two, and *too* must be used correctly or meaning will not be exchanged.

Another example of American grammar rules in the use of the words "less" and "fewer". You are standing on line at the grocery store and you see this sign: 10 items or less.

- 10 items or less is incorrect.
- 10 items or fewer is correct.

Fewer is used for countable things like your groceries. Less is used for mass nouns as in this sentence "you need less salt in your diet."

Here is a fun example: Winston Tastes Good Like a Cigarette Should.

One of the most recognizable commercial slogans ever devised is *Winston taste Good Like a Cigarette Should.* Grammatically this sentence is incorrect. The correct usage would be *Winston Tastes Good **as** a Cigarette should.*

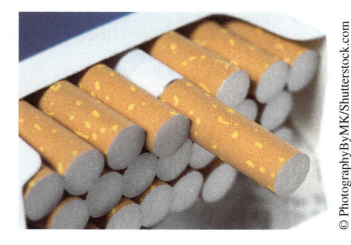

The Ad agency that came up with this slogan knew that they had made a grammatical *faux pas,* but also knew that such a mistake would generate buzz. And did it ever. Wander around the Internet and read about this "controversy." Some TV newsreaders refused to say the slogan at all because they knew it was incorrect and did not want to sound like they didn't know that. At one point the company changed the slogan to read "Winston taste Good Like As a Cigarette Should", which is correct. That generated another round of buzz.

Spelling

English has spelling rules. These rules are broken with abandon.

I before E except after C or sounding like A as in neighbor or weigh.

U follows Q.

Because you know English spelling you can read this:

"Aoccdrnig to a rscheearch at CmabrigdeUinervtisy, it deosn'tmttaer in wahtoredr the ltteers in a wrod are, the olnyiprmoatnttihng is taht the frist and lsatltteers be at the rghitpclae. The rset can be a toatlmses and you can sitllraed it wouthitporbelm. Tihs is bcuseae the huamnmniddeos not raederveylteter by istlef, but the wrod as a wlohe." *(www.physicsforum, 2017)*

Ablaut Reduplication

If you ever wondered why you say ding dong and not dong ding, this is why. English has rules about word order. Dong Ding doesn't sound right to you because the rule is "the first word has to have the "I" in it". If there are three words in the group then the "a" comes next and then the "o."

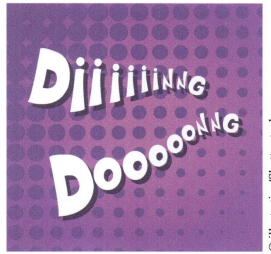

- Sing song
- Hip Hop
- Chit-chat
- Ping Pong

The next part of the rule has to do with how adjectives are lined up in sentences. We say "little green men," not "green little men" because "green little men" just sounds wrong.

LANGUAGE IS SYMBOLIC

The word is not the thing is how we generally describe what we mean by the symbolic nature of language. The symbolic nature of language is what makes it so difficult for you to choose the right word to convey your meaning. Because language is symbolic words take on multiple meanings, gain new meanings, and lose old meanings.

Words represent the **meaning** we intend to convey.

- The word *water* is not wet.
- The word *sun* is not bright and shiny.
- The word *yes* is not in itself an agreement. The agreement is your actions, thoughts, or beliefs.

Here is an example of how "the word is not the thing."

Define Rhoop: An exercise in meaning is symbolic

Write down your definition of the word "Rhoop." Then we will break up into dyads to share that definition. Then into groups of four. Share the definition. Finally, we will discuss the definition together.

Just so you know: Rhoop* is not a real word in the sense that we understand words.

Rhoop Definition:

Dyads Definition:

Group of Four Definition:

What is the same or different about these definitions?

What you undoubtedly discovered is that no two people have the same definition of this word. That is because the word is not the thing. If it were then we all would have had the same meaning for *Rhoop*. We would have "known" what it was even if we could not describe it. We would have had very similar explanations of the meaning.

*If you Google *Rhoop* you will discover that the first page or so of hits refer to a proper name used by CS Lewis in *The Chronicles of Narnia*. And that is about it.

LANGUAGE AND MEANING

Your own experience tells you that individual words, phrases, sentences, and paragraphs can have multiple meanings. The meaning we attach to words and phrases is developed from a variety of different sources. We will become better communicators, if we understand how word-meanings come into being.

Words have Power

© Kunal Mehta/Shutterstock.com

The Meaning of Words is Arbitrary

People decide what words will represent what things. This is one of the reasons words have so many meanings.

- What does the expression "You feel me" mean?
- Why do we call a writing implement *pen* and not *cow*?

There is no reason why these words and phrases mean what they do. Groups of people decide what words and phrase will mean. When the meaning is generally accepted then the word has that meaning. However, a word or phrase does not have to have a generally accepted meaning for it mean some specific to you. Your small group of friends, your family, your workplace could all assign meanings to words and phrases that become part of how you speak and are understood among those groups.

Here are a few examples of how we assign meanings to words and phrases.

Portmanteau Words

Merriam-Webster defines portmanteau as a word or morpheme whose form and meaning are derived from a blending of two or more distinct forms.

Motel. A combination of motor and hotel.
Chilax. A combination of chill out and relax.
Hangry. A combination of *hungry* and *angry*. It has the specific meaning of being angry because you are hungry.

Portmanteaus begin their lives as neologisms.

Neologisms

Neologisms are "new words." They are words invented to express ideas or things that did not previously exist.

Telegenic means . . .? You look good on TV. It is a combination of television and photogenic. Before the advent of TV this word was not needed. After the Nixon/Kennedy debates it was.

MacGyver means . . . what?

Is this word a noun or a verb? Where did it come from?

How would you use it in a sentence? * Give it a try. Use this word is a sentence based on your understanding of what it actually means or what you think it means.

The all-time best neologism is "beclown." "Beclown" means you turn yourself into a clown. Use— "You have beclowned yourself by making that ridiculous charge."

Now, this is not really a neologism as the word has been around for a long time. The Oxford English Dictionary includes a 1609 quote, *O wretch, O Lob, who would be thus beclown'd?* (S. ROWLANDS *Whole Crew Kind Gossips* 24) that tells us this word has been around for 400 years.

But words come in and out of fashion. For us this is a new word.

The Urban Dictionary has this definition:

Verb. To make a complete idiot of oneself in public. To behave or speak in such a way, or to make a comment or express an opinion that is so profoundly witless, senseless, and obtuse, that you have forever after defined yourself as a person of comical value only. Never to be taken seriously again. Of worth only as an object of ridicule and derision.

This web site has a fun list of neologisms. It includes a contest run by the *Washington Post* that asked people to invent new words for modern phenomena.

https://www.vappingo.com/word-blog/great-examples-of-neologisms/

© Elnur/Shutterstock.com

Jargon and slang

Hip means . . . it's a body part. Slang-wise, however, it means you are with it, you know the score.

Rip off means . . . to tear something away of course, but over time it has also come to mean stealing in some form or another.

Cool means . . . not cold or hot. But we all know that it also means being hip, groovy, and far-out. Fashionable. Good.

© awesome design studio/Shutterstock.com

Product Names

What word do we use when asking for a tissue?

What word do we use when explaining that we are making photocopies?

What word do we use when we explain that we are looking up something on the Internet?

© TeddyandMia/Shutterstock.com

And the answers are: Kleenex, Xerox, and Google.

That's right. We are using product names. These names are shortcuts, stand–ins for an entire category of thing.

The use of *Google* to mean conducting an Internet search came into general use very quickly. Surprisingly so in some ways.

Take the Portmanteau or Neologism Challenge

Invent and define three new words that describe recent understandings of the world. An example: **affluenza** (a combination of affluence and influenza): The guilt or lack of motivation experienced by people who have made or inherited large amounts of money (vapingo.com).

1)

2)

3)

The Meaning of Words is Learned

Language must be taught. We don't have language in our heads when we are born, but we do have a universal grammar. Our understanding of grammar pre-dates our language acquisition. We learn language from a variety of sources as we grow into adults.

Because meanings of words are learned, not all people will learn exactly the same meaning for them. There are many influences on meaning and those affect how people use language.

© kozirsky/Shutterstock.com

Meaning by Denotation

One of the ways we learn the meaning of words is by going to the dictionary. There you will find the denotative definitions of the words you use. These definitions are the ones universally accepted by the speakers of that particular language.

According to the Oxford English dictionary the English language has 171,476 words in current use, and 47,156 obsolete words that are part of the language but are no longer in use. These 218,632 words have a combined 615,100 definitions (OED, 2017).

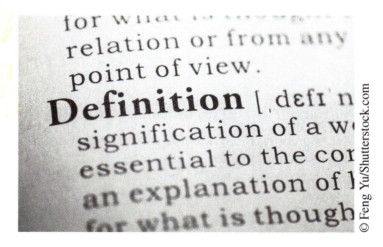

© Feng Yu/Shutterstock.com

As you can see most words have multiple definitions. Here are the top 10 according to Dictionary.com:

- "Set" has 464 definitions in the *Oxford English Dictionary*. "Run" runs a distant second, with 396.
- Rounding out the top 10 are "go" with 368, "take" with 343, "stand" with 334, "get" with 289, "turn" with 288, "put" with 268, "fall" with 264, and "strike" with 250.

Denotative meanings change over time.

- The word "NICE" has been in use in English for over 700 years.
- Between 1300 and now "nice" has meant: foolish, wanton, lazy, strange, coy, modest, refined, precise, subtle, slender, critical, attentive, accurate, appetizing, and agreeable.

Meaning by Connotation

Words also gain meaning on an individual level. Your feelings, experiences, and associations with words give them a secondary meaning that is personal to you. These meanings are not shared by the wider world. This is why it is so easy to offend people with your language choice. You cannot know how people feel about words unless they tell you.

It is the feeling one has about what a word means that leads to euphemisms and the language use we call Political Correctness and Triggers. We sometimes call such words red or green flag words. Red flag words evoke a negative emotional response. Green flag words evoke a positive emotional response.

LET'S PLAY

What is your favorite word and why?

What is your least favorite word and why?

What is a trigger word for you?

What is your favorite euphemism and what does it mean?

Meaning Is Abstract

Abstract language is general in nature. It doesn't refer to specific things. Its application is more universal.

The word *vehicle,* for example, can refer to any type or mode of transportation. It is more abstract than car, bus, or truck.

Words like love, patriotism, and loyalty are also abstract.

In English, we use the word love to refer to anything from "I love that color" to "I love my new coat" to "I love my dog" to "I love my spouse." Each of these uses of love has a different meaning.

© Irina_QQQ/Shutterstock.com

In Greek, there is a more concrete way to speak of love. *Phileo* is the love between friends and would not be confused with *eros*, which is erotic or romantic love, or *agape* which is spiritual love.

Words step down from being quite unspecific to quite concrete.

Meaning Is Concrete

Some words have specific meanings. The more concrete the language choice the more specific the meaning becomes. The more specific the language gets the fewer meanings can be assigned to it. Concrete language is more likely to produce understanding as the possibility of misinterpreting the symbol is less. Words such as

- Lamborghini Aventador
- Hourly wage-earner
- Soulmate

© italianestro/Shutterstock.com

are more concrete than vehicle, working class, and lover.

Abstract to Concrete

Fill in the boxes from most abstract to most concrete for the following concepts. Have fun. The point here is to see how concrete you can get and to maximize understanding.

Concept	Most Abstract					Most Concrete
Your address						
Chair						
Your name						

Meaning Is in Context

When we say that meaning is based on context we are referring to two things: the communication situation and something called collocation.

Language is influenced by **the communication situation** in which that language is used. All language conforms to the context in which it is found. Nonverbal cues do, too, by the way.

© AlexRoz/Shutterstock.com

- The example "how are you" is a good one. It means one thing if you are on the street and something completely different if you are visiting in the hospital.
- The passage of time plays a role here as well. Language changes over time. What was once offensive is now not. Once swearing was not allowed on broadcast TV. Now it is.

Language is also influenced by something called **collocation.** Collocation refers to where a word appears in relationship to the words around it.

- Definition: collocation is a familiar grouping of words, especially words that habitually appear together and thereby convey meaning by association. Collocational range refers to the set of items that typically accompany a word (Nordquist 2016).
- Example: Up
  - ❏ Sit up
  - ❏ Grow up
  - ❏ Grown up
  - ❏ Push up
  - ❏ Get up
  - ❏ Close up
  - ❏ Open up
  - ❏ Follow up
  - ❏ Start up
  - ❏ Dry up
  - ❏ Clam up
  - ❏ Look up

Each one of these word groups means something different even though *up* appears in each one. The context—the word or words around up affect the meaning of this tiny word *up*.

English speakers also group words to convey specific meaning.

- Pouring rain
- Scenic view
- Winding road
- Blissfully ignorant
- Bright idea
- Talk freely

Collocations "just sound right" to the speaker. You say, "Let's get some fast food." You would never say, "Let's get some speedy food."

Meaning Is in People

Your speaking patterns are unique to you.

You do not sound like anyone else in the world.

You are creative in your use of words and how you put those words together to form your verbal message.

© Rawpixel.com/Shutterstock.com

You might make up new words or use old words with a new definition. After a while those around you become used to how you use language and understand you. You fashion your own meaning for words even though you know the generally accepted meanings. You receive the meaning of words through the learning process, but then create your own meaning for them.

The meanings of messages are derived from what the speaker thinks and feels and what the receiver thinks and feels. No two people will derive the same meaning from a message. So, while the meanings will come close to being the same that is the best we can do.

A good example of this is the concept of time. Each of us has a different idea of what time is and what expressions denoting time mean. Part of this is culture-based, part experience, and part family.

What do you mean by:

- I'll be done in a minute.
- This will only take a second.
- I'll be there shortly.
- Don't be late.

We can solve many interpersonal problems by explaining exactly what we mean when we use these expressions.

CULTURE AND LANGUAGE

Language is used to support and transmit cultural history, values, beliefs, attitudes, and acceptable or unacceptable behavior. Language is a vehicle by which culture is sustained from one generation to the next. Even if that language is, for example, English, one can readily see how British English and American English express the differences between these cultures.

Everyday word choice is different:

© robuart/Shutterstock.com

- American English
  - ❑ Truck
  - ❑ Subway
  - ❑ Elevator

- British English
  - ❑ Lorry
  - ❑ Underground
  - ❑ Lift

Even deeper differences exist with words like *crown* and *royal*. To the British these words encompass the entirety of their experiences of monarchy and their monarchy in particular. Americans do not use or understand these words in the same way.

Here is another example of how language is informed by culture: The word **BISCUIT**.

- You are a cabinet maker: A biscuit joins two pieces of wood together.
- You are a southerner: You make and eat biscuits.
- You are from England: A biscuit is a cracker-like food.
- You are Yosemite Sam: "My biscuits are burning."

© Marie C Fields/Shutterstock.com

The importance of language as a means of communication is not the same in every culture. Some cultures value verbal skills more highly than others. In America, it is important to be able to speak well. Fluency is a prized virtue in America.

Other cultures put more emphasis on nonverbal cues as a means of communicating. Cultures are pegged along a continuum of High Context (nonverbal emphasis) to Low Context (verbal emphasis).

High Context Cultures

High context cultures place an emphasis on nonverbal communication. These cultures spend less time speaking and more time assessing nonverbal cues. Such cultures use fewer words when communicating.

Examples: Japanese, Arab, and Greek.

© Kheng Guan Toh /Shutterstock.com

Low Context Cultures

These cultures put an emphasis on verbal communication. Such cultures use many words to convey messages. Obviously, people in these cultures spend more time speaking.

Examples: German, Swiss, and American.

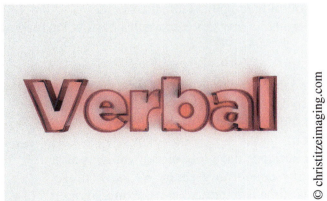

© christitzeimaging.com /Shutterstock.com

Language and Culture Reflect each Other

How a culture views its language tells you a lot about that culture. For example, a language reflects a culture's multicultural nature. American English is a multicultural language. It started out that way with a mix of northern European languages and then added French, Greek, Latin, and then on and on.

American English is perfectly happy to take whatever words work, regardless of that word's origin and incorporate it into itself. These words are referred to as "loanwords." And there are a surprising number of them in American English. Check out this link for some interesting loanwords: http://www.englishleap.com/vocabulary/foreign-language-words

The French, on the other hand, are very protective of their language. It is an important cultural artifact for the French and so they guard their language from outside influences. This article discusses the struggle to preserve French from outside influences. https://www.thelocal.fr/20130204/french-language-franglais-culture-paris-english-protect-promote

Language Reflects What a Culture Values

If you study a language long enough you come to know what the people who use that language find important and what they do not.

Euphemisms are used to make taboo subjects appropriate for general conversation. You can tell what a culture finds taboo by studying its euphemisms.

Death, sex, pregnancy, and bathroom issues all have multiple euphemisms. These are embarrassing subjects for general discussion, or at least they used to be in American culture, so American English as developed multiple ways of mitigating that embarrassment.

Here are a few more examples of how language reflects cultural values.

Time

Americans value time and let time dominate their lives. And if you don't think that is true count the number of clocks you have in your kitchen.

Americans have lots of euphemisms and proverbs concerning time. We have those because time is important to us. Examples are:

Time flies when you are having fun.

A stitch in time saves nine.

Time and tides wait for no man.
Time is money.
He who has time has life.
Time heals all wounds.

Americans look at time as a commodity. It can be saved, spent, you own it. Not everyone looks at time like this.

Baseball

Baseball may no longer be America's sport but it still dominates the American consciousness. American English is full of sayings, euphemisms and allusions to baseball. What this tells you is that baseball is part of how we communicate as Americans. You may be completely uninterested in the sport but you talk like you are playing the game every day, all day long.

© zsolt_uveges/Shutterstock.com

Wow, that guy is way out in left field.
A ballpark figure on the cost of the party is $3000.
You are batting 1000. Great job.
That speech was a grand slam.
With that grade, I was back in the ballgame.
Did you make it to first base last night?
And then I was thrown a curve ball.
My boss is playing hardball with me about my raise.

Celebrating the Holiday Time between Thanksgiving and New Year

If you look at a calendar for the year, oh let's say, 1956, you will find Thanksgiving and Christmas are the only holidays indicated from the end of November to the end of December. This tells you that these holidays were the only important holidays back then.

© Elena Shashkina/Shutterstock.com

A look at a modern calendar will show the following:
Thanksgiving
Hanukkah
Ramadan (if the year is correct)
Kwanza
The Winter Solstice

Greeting cards follow suit. Now you will see

- Season's Greetings
- Happy Holidays

- Merry Christmas
- Happy Hanukkah
- Happy Kwanza

What this show is that America is pluralistic when it comes to religious faith. In mono-religious countries such diversity of express will not be found.

By the way, if you Google "holiday greetings" what you get is the Christmas holiday. This is a perfect example of what this culture thinks important even though it is trying to become more diverse.

Language reflects changes in cultures

Words change meaning as the culture changes. Words fall in and out of fashion. New words are produced. Old words are mothballed.

Swear words are a fun example of how this works. Have you seen the books or gone to the websites that teach you how to swear and hurl insults like and Elizabethan? (*Hurl insults* is a collocation, by the way. One would never throw an insult.) These books take the swear words out of Shakespeare's plays and other Elizabethan literature and then devise interesting ways for you to insult or swear at people without them knowing it. For example,

Thou art a fobbing, hedge-born malt-worm.

It's fun, but doesn't mean anything. These words are not considered swear words or insulting anymore, so they have lost their ability to shock and dismay.

This web site should help you learn this valuable skill: http://www.museangel.net/insult.htm

The TV show *Firefly* hit the airwaves in 2002. It was still not possible in 2002, on broadcast TV anyway, to use any of George Carlin's "Seven Words You Can't Say on TV." In order to include swear words in the show, the series creator, Joss Whedon, incorporated Chinese into the English spoken by the culture in which the show was set, including Chinese swear words. Of course, these words passed the censors. Unless a culture views a word as taboo, the word has no power to offend.

We are well passed this now. The number of swear words you can't hear on TV these days is not a lot.

LANGUAGE AND PERCEPTION

So, there is a big dispute among linguists about how language and perception interact with each other. How much does language influence our perception of the world around us and conversely how much does perception influence our language choice? These questions continue to plague those interested in how language and perception interact. We should be those people, too.

There are those who subscribe to the Linguistic Relativity Hypothesis (LRH). LRH suggests that people's worldview is constrained by their language

use. Others in various fields of study dispute this hypothesis, most importantly the great linguist John McWhorter.

Jack Vance uses the context of a science fiction novel to map out how the LRH might work in real life. In his 1958 book *The Language of Pao*, Vance invents worlds, Pao and Breakness, which develop differently because of how their languages work. The language spoken on Pao has no verbs, no adjectives, and no words of comparison—good, better, best. This leads the culture to be lazy and uncreative. Breakness has an individualistic language which focuses on self. There is no one word for "I" because everyone is an individual "I." One culture was passive and one aggressive and you can tell which is which.

The proverb "To a hammer everything is a nail" sums up how the LRH works.
For a good, short explanation of all of this, go to this link:
http://www.linguisticsociety.org/resource/language-and-thought
So what do you think? How do language and perception affect one another?

How Language and Perception Interact

Names

Names are more than just designations for people, places, and things. Names shape the way we see ourselves and the way others see us. Names:

© Miceking/Shutterstock.com

    Indicate Relationships
    Indicate Social Status
    Reveal Stereotypes
    Are our brand

Tell Us Your Names

List below all the names by which you are called:

Now list who you allow to use which names:

How you chose to call yourself says a lot about who you are to the people around you.

- Do you have people call you by your first, middle, or last name?
- Do you prefer people to use your title and last name if you don't know them well?

- Do you use a diminutive of your name? A nickname?
- Do you use a different, more formal name in public settings and a more casual name in private settings?

The choices you make here will indicate to the people around you what kind of relationship you wish to have with them. Context plays a role as well. We are less formal at home than in public. There was a time in the United States when husbands and wives called each other Mr. and Mrs. with last name, in the family setting. This practice was never standard across the culture and continues to strike us as an odd and distant way for intimates to interact.

- Title and last name shows formality
- Using your family nickname shows closeness
- Using a designation like "sweetie" shows closeness which is why you don't necessarily like it when the wait staff at the diner calls you honey.

We stereotype people based on the names they have been given.

The Name Game

Here is a list of names. List five characteristics you associate with these names

Sally

Cinnamon

Tarik

Poindexter

Why did you make the choices you did?

Our Brand

Impression management includes how we call ourselves in both private and public. Our impression management is our brand and all brands need a good name.

© theromb/Shutterstock.com

Our brand may be a portmanteau name. We may not personally have one of these but we know people who do. Portmanteau names are singular

- J.Lo (Jennifer Lopez)
- ScarJo (Scarlett Johansson)
- T-Rex (Rex Tillerson)

or plural

- Bennifer (Ben Affleck and Jennifer Lopez)
- Brangelina (Brad Pitt and Angelina Jolie)

Your Brand

Now make up your own Portmanteau name:

What does your portmanteau name say about your brand?

Our brand may be a nickname or a title or a completely made up name. Think of the rock star Prince who eventually changed his name to a symbol so everyone had to call him "the rock star formally known as Prince" when they wanted to talk about him. By the way, Prince's given name was Prince Rogers Nelson.

In the Golden Age of Hollywood, movie studios routinely changed the names of their actors. If the actor had a foreign-sounding name, a difficult to pronounce name, or a name that did not reflect the type of star the studio wanted the actor to be, the name was changed. And this is what happened.

Marilyn Monroe	Norma Jean Baker
Tony Curtis	Bernie Schwartz
Kirk Douglas	Issur Danielovitch Demsky
Judy Garland	Francis Gumm
Michael Caine	Maurice Micklewhite
Rock Hudson	Leroy Harold Scherer, Jr.

Rappers and Hip-Hop artists rarely go by their birth names straight up. Often there is a change of some sort or the rappers abandon their real names for something completely different. These names are brands the artists are promoting.

Jay-Z	Shawn Corey Carpenter
2PAC	Tupac Shakur
Notorious B.I.G.	Christopher George Latore Wallace
Wiz Khalifa	Cameron JibrilThomaz
50 Cent	Curtis James Jackson III
Nicki Minaj	Onika Tanya Maraj

Some famous people are known by titles. These titles are given them by the culture to explain that person's importance to society.

The Great Emancipator	Abraham Lincoln
The Great Commoner	William Jennings Bryan
Le Corbusier (The Raven)	Charles-Edouard Jeanneret (famous architect)

And it's not just people. Businesses spend a great deal of money choosing and marketing names for their products. Businesses hire lawyers to research names to make sure the name doesn't exist in the real world to avoid lawsuits. Choosing the wrong name for a product can create headaches for companies and cost them a lot of money.

- In 1997, Reeboks had to recall 18,000 boxes of a $57.99 women's sneaker because they had foolishly named the sneaker *Incubus*. An incubus is a demon who sexually assaults women in their sleep. Not a good choice for Reeboks.
- 666 cold remedy has a similar problem. 666 is the number of Satan. Who thought that was a good idea?

Descriptors

The words we choose to use to describe the world around us reflect our perceptions at that point in time.

What does today's weather look like to you? When you describe your thoughts about the weather to another you are revealing your perceptions of it.

A good example of how language reflects and creates perceptions is political campaigns. Here is a list. What is the first thing you notice?

- Representative Jones rallied the troops for one last get out the vote effort.
- There is a war on the middle class.
- The speech was the opening salvo in what may prove to be a hard-fought battle.
- Moderates find themselves in a no-mans land when it comes to political parties.

Each sentence employs a word or phrase taken straight from the language of war. What does that tell you about how we view politics? This language use encourages people to see politics, not as an arena of opposing ideas, but as personal combat of right against wrong. And in war the goal is to win at all costs.

Then we come to describing people. The language we use to describe others tells those others what we think about them.

- You indicate your perceptions of others by the words you use about them.
- Society has become very aware of how perception of individuals is influenced by the language used to describe them.
- News organizations have style manuals that indicate the preferred way of addressing individuals and groups.

Immigration

What language can be used to describe those who come to the United States without going through the process the government has instituted for entering the country? List three or four.

Know explain the perception created by each of your choices.

Think of how you describe your best friend to others. Are the characteristics you use upbeat and positive, neutral or negative? What is the first thing you say about your best friend when describing the friend to others? What you decide to say about your friend tells your listener the following:

- What you think about your friend.
- What you want the listener to think about your friend.
- What your description says about you as a friend.
- What your description says about your understanding of your relationship with the best friend.

CREDIBILITY AND STATUS

The power of speech to influence people's perception of individual status and credibility is very real. Remember that the higher your status is the more likely people will want to believe you, follow you, like you.

The words we use and the way we pronounce them have a huge effect on people. Your ideas are more likely to be accepted the more precise you are in the words you use. The more educated you sound the more likely it is that people will listen to you.

Of course, credibility and status perceptions are both context-based and culture-based. If you want to exchange meaning with others, you need to speak their language. That means that you develop the ability to adapt to the language use and speech patterns of the people with whom you are conversing.

It is important for you to have a large vocabulary. This vocabulary will include standard language use plus slang and jargon.

- You establish credibility and status with your friends by using language that has been accepted in the friendship group.
- You establish credibility and status on your job by using the jargon of that business.

Change It Up

List three or four words you use with each group that you don't use with the others. What does your list tell you?

Family	Friends	Work

INFLUENCES ON OUR LANGUAGE CHOICE

No two people in your Interpersonal Communication class have exactly the same vocabulary. That is because the language you all know and use has been influenced in different ways than that of your classmates. Here is a list of influences on your language choice.

Cultural Influence

You belong to many cultural groups. These groups include the overarching culture of America, your family, your sports team, your ethnic group, and any other group you can think of.

Each of these groups speaks its own language. Even if the same words are used, the culture in which this language is used changes the meaning.

© ESB Professional/Shutterstock.com

- ■ Your college has its own language.
    - ❑ Matriculate
    - ❑ Bursar
    - ❑ GPA
- ■ Your family has specific ways of using language
    - ❑ Private language
        - ● Made up words
            - ○ CYK (consider yourself kissed)
            - ○ Dubbydee (diaper thrown over the shoulder and used when burping a baby)
        - ● Family nicknames
            - ○ Tootles
            - ○ BoBoo
    - ❑ Naming grandparents
        - ● Nana and Papa
        - ● Opa and Muti
        - ● Granny and Gramps
- ■ Your ethnic group includes first and second language in its everyday speech.
    - ❑ You have chutzpah. (Yiddish)
    - ❑ That's part of the zeitgeist. (German)

Geographic Influence

Different regions of the country use different words to describe the same thing. In fact, you can pretty much tell where someone is from by the words they use. For example, what do you call a drink that is made with milk, ice cream, and syrup?

- In New York, it's a milk shake.
- In Massachusetts, it's a frappe.
- In Rhode Island, it's a cabinet.

This influence holds true throughout the world. In some places, this may mean no shared language at all. Papua New Guinea has 839 indigenous languages. Most are tribal languages that are not shared with other groups.

Test the New York Times to see if their quiz answer agrees with where you have lived.

Take this quiz and see how you do: http://www.nytimes.com/interactive/2013/12/20/sunday-review/dialect-quiz-map.html?r=8004485104001048000200800140400040j00j10020200b000j&_r=0

Education Influence

What we study, whether in school or on our own, influences our language choice. Just going to college does the same.

The longer you stay in school and the more you read the larger your vocabulary will become.

Specialized Language

What is your major?

List 5–10 words that are specific to your major that you are sure others in the class will not know or will ascribe a different meaning to than the meaning you know.

1)
2)
3)
4)
5)
6)
7)
8)
9)
10)

Share your list. What do you learn from this exercise?

LANGUAGE BARRIERS TO COMMUNICATION

It should be obvious by now that word choice can create barriers to the exchange of meaning. Here are some examples of the kind of barriers you need to watch out for.

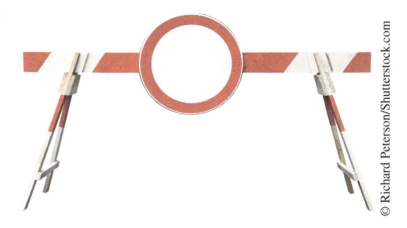

© Richard Peterson/Shutterstock.com

Allness

Definition: The belief that what you say about something is all there is to say on the subject—there is nothing else to learn.

All statements are limited by your specific knowledge. Something else can always be said. It is not possible to have all the information necessary to make a decision. But you do the best you can and that includes saying you don't know all there is to know.

© Mohd KhairilX/Shutterstock.com

Bypassing

Definition: Believing you understand the message when you do not. You assume the listener has the same meaning for words and ideas that you do. Bypassing takes two forms.

- When people use different words, and give them the same meaning.
- When two people use the same word, but give it different meanings.

© Nuamfolio/Shutterstock.com

Here is the all-time classic example of bypassing.
https://youtu.be/K0Jg7pvVzKk?list=RDbpxkyTc9Z38 as performed by Jimmy Fallon, Billy Crystal, and Jerry Seinfeld.

Downward Talk

Definition: Putting a listener in the one-down position through language use. You put yourself above others through language use.

Examples of downward talk.

- Assuming greater intelligence—"You probably won't understand this…"
- Explaining to someone how that person should feel—"Don't feel that way. It is not helpful."
- Interrupting others.
- Purposely using language in a complex and pseudo-intellectual way to encourage people to feel stupid.

Downward talk is the whole principle behind racist and sexist language. It is the attempt to make people feel bad about themselves while making the speaker sound superior.

Fact/Inference Confusion

Definition: Mistaking inferences/opinions for facts.

Facts are observed reality.

Sun rises in the east.

Water is wet.

The Earth revolves around the Sun.

Inferences are assumptions you make from what you see.

Crossed arms show that a person is angry.

I got a "D" because the professor does not like me.

Fact/Inference

There is a truck parked in my neighbor's driveway. It is white and has "Smiling Doug's Electric" painted on the side. The truck has been parked in the driveway for three hours. I know because I saw it pull in and have been watching it ever since.

Play Sherlock Holmes. What can you deduce from this paragraph? What are the facts in evidence?

What can you infer from this paragraph?

Discuss.

In-Group Talk

Definition: Language shared by a small group within the larger society is sometimes called as jargon.

© Philip Date/Shutterstock.com

You are used to using certain words and phrases among yourselves that others outside your family, friendship group, profession, or even company may not know.

Using this type of language is fine within your group, but it is a difficult thing when you bring it out of the group into everyday use.

In-group talk can be beneficial to group cohesion. In fact, one of the ways groups promote cohesion is to develop language that only the group knows.

However, using in-group talk can impede communication.

- Messages are not understood.
- People are made to feel stupid and left out.
- People are sensitive and they may think you are trying to make them feel stupid when you are merely using the language you are used to. Be careful here.

Your In-Group Talk

Choose one group you belong to and list five or six words used by that group that other will not understand.

1)

2)

3)

4)

5)

6)

Share and discuss.

Labeling

Definition: This is the tendency to view people, objects, and events by either how they are labeled or by how others talk about them.

What you need to do is to take the labels into account, but understand that these are not the only way to view people, places, and things. Remember our discussion regarding perception and language use.

Lying

Definition: Telling a deliberate untruth.

Is there any need to discuss this? Lying is wrong most of the time. It hampers communication because it distorts meaning and put erroneous information into the communication situation.

Besides, it is never safe.

- It is very hard to tell a long consist lie.
- Eventually the lie will be discovered.
- Once lost, trust is very hard to find again.

Polarization

Definition: Describing people, places, and things in either/or terms.

Polarized language encourages people to think there is no middle ground; there is no nuance to life.

You look at the world in terms of opposites and describe the world as one or the other.

Opposites

Give me the opposite of the following: hot, short, legal, smart.

That's not very hard.

Now give the midpoint of each.

Not so easy. But there is a middle ground for many things and we should be able to find it. This is especially true when dealing with people on contentious issues. The attempt to find a middle ground to a problem can help ease a difficult situation or at least keep an argument from degenerating into "Yes you did." "No I didn't."

And yes, there are issues, idea, concepts that have no middle group. Many of these are moral in nature. What do you think? Where is there no middle ground?

Static Evaluation

Definition: The tendency to ignore that things change over time.

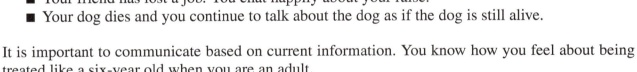

You can't step into the same river twice (a saying attributed to Heraclitus) has come to mean that the world is in constant flux. It is always changing.

Yet there are times when we use language that indicates we do not accept the changing nature of the world.

- Your Mom still talks to you like a six-year old.
- Your friend has lost a job. You chat happily about your raise.
- Your dog dies and you continue to talk about the dog as if the dog is still alive.

It is important to communicate based on current information. You know how you feel about being treated like a six-year old when you are an adult.

WHAT CAN I DO TO IMPROVE MY VERBAL SKILLS?

The barriers mentioned above can be overcome by observing the following.

Be Precise in Your Word Choice

The more accurate you are in your word choice the more likely you are to exchange meaning.

Example 1: You are asked if the coffee is hot.

- If the coffee is hot but drinkable by a reasonable person then it is not scalding. It may not even be hot. Find the word that best describes it.

Example 2: I misplaced your book indicates that the book may yet be found.

- If you really lost the book you need to say, "I lost your book."
- Your friend will then know that the book is gone for good.

The More Concrete the Better

Avoid using flowery language that is not easily understood. Go the Winston Churchill route. Avoid multisyllabic words.

"I am having a metaphysical experience here" does not convey as much as "I see a dead people!"

Avoid Allness Language

Words like "always," "never," "every" are seldom the case.

- It does not always rain on one's day off.
- It is unlikely that your friend is never on time.

ONE SIZE DOES NOT FIT ALL

Use Words Correctly

Using words incorrectly muddies the meaning and makes you lose credibility in the eyes of the listener.

If you want the listener to know that you have an **eminently** popular policy and you say you have an **imminently** popular policy, you are likely to have trouble.

A **misnomer** is a wrong name or designation. It is not a generic mistake.

© inspiron.dell.vector/Shutterstock.com

Avoid Cliches, Euphemism and Ambiguities

Cliches are sayings that are very familiar and therefore lack punch. They do not make your message more interesting.

Euphemisms are phrases that allow taboo topics to be mentioned in general conversation.

Ambiguities are words that cause us to be confused. What was really meant?

Avoiding this language use makes your message unique to you. Also, such usage is highly culture-specific. One of the most difficult things to learn is another culture's euphemisms and clichés.

© TypoArt BS/Shutterstock.com

*From the Rice University Neologism Database we find:

MacGyver, noun: analogy

One who can use materials in novel ways; an informal name given to one who can use materials for many untraditional purposes in creative ways. Usually one who is able to use his or her skills in high-pressure situations. Originated from a television show about a man who used his science and wits, instead of violence, to solve problems (Kemmer, 2008).

Chapter 6

"Yippie- Ki- yay. . ."

—John MaClane, *Die Hard*

A Discussion of Vocalics

In the last chapter, we discussed how words begin the exchange of meaning. In this chapter, we will look at HOW those words are said. The topic of this chapter is Vocalics. Vocalics is a funny thing. Because words are involved, you might think of it as verbal communication. Actually, it is a type of nonverbal communication. This nonverbal cue deserves its own chapter because it is a bridge cue between verbal and nonverbal.

By themselves, words have meaning, but that is only part of the story. How you say the words you use conveys another layer of meaning. Do this:

Say "I went to LA". Now say this sentence

- Putting the emphasis on the first word. Now the second. Now the third. Now the fourth.
- As if you are asking a question.
- As if you are annoyed because the person you are speaking to doesn't get it.
- As if you are being sarcastic.

See what happens? The volume, rate, intonation, and pitch of your voice changes the meaning.

Don't speak to me in that tone of voice. You have heard that, perhaps many times. We know that how something is said is important. It may be even more important than the words themselves. Having control of your voice, understanding how your voice conveys meaning and learning correct articulation, pronunciation, and enunciation will help you make the right choices in a given communication situation.

HOW THE VOICE WORKS

You have an anatomy that makes it possible for you to speak. Notice something about that system. The picture here is of the respiratory system—the system that makes it possible for you to breathe. Providing nothing goes wrong with it, you have the ability to form sounds and make them understandable to others through using this system. Interestingly, speech is not this system's primary function. Speech is an overlaid function on the respiratory system. It is, luckily, an overlay that works. Here is what you need to articulate the sounds in whatever language you speak.

- Air
- Diaphragm
- Lungs
- Larynx
- Vocal folds
- Epiglottis
- Uvula
- Hard and soft palate
- Teeth
- Tongue
- Nasal cavity

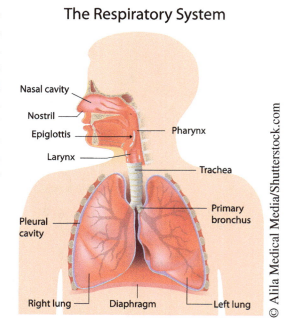

The Respiratory System

Nasal cavity
Nostril
Epiglottis
Pharynx
Larynx
Trachea
Primary bronchus
Pleural cavity
Right lung
Diaphragm
Left lung

© Alila Medical Media/Shutterstock.com

You will notice that the picture is missing something. Take a look at this:

What you are looking at is a picture of your larynx and vocal cords or folds. These are necessary for speech. People with cancer of the larynx have this whole apparatus excised. Without learning how to breathe through the hole in the throat or without the aid of an artificial larynx and vocal folds these cancer sufferers cannot speak.

So, what happens when you speak? Here is what happens:

The Larynx and Vocal Cords

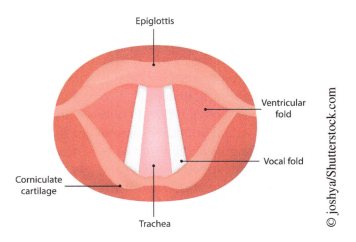

© joshya/Shutterstock.com

- You inhale air. At this point, your diaphragm rises and flattens, pushing your ribcage up and out.
- The air travels through the larynx and starts your vocal folds vibrating. The speed of the air and the length and thickness of the vocal folds produce pitch. The longer and thicker the vocal folds, the lower the voice will be.
  - ❏ Men's vocal folds are long and thick.
  - ❏ Women's vocal folds are shorter and thinner.
  - ❏ Children's vocal folds are very short and thin.
- At this point, you are creating sound (phonation) but it doesn't mean anything.
- This sound then passes up to the articulators
  - ❏ The pharyngeal cavity (a little tube that helps with resonance).
  - ❏ The oral (the inside of your mouth).
  - ❏ The nasal (your nose and surrounding cavities).
- Now you are ready to pronounce sounds.

I know what you're thinking. You're thinking "I thought I was taking Interpersonal Communication not A and P!" You are in luck because you are taking Interpersonal. Ok, then. Why do you have to know this? As with every aspect of communication, you need to make choices and you need to make them well. The more you know about how your voice works, the more control you can have over it. The more control you have over it, the better you will be at making effective choices.

Using your voice to its greatest affect means learning about

- Articulation.
- Pronunciation.
- Enunciation.

These three components act together to make intelligible speech.

Articulation

Articulation is the formation of sounds using the speech organs. Here is a picture of your articulators. Oh, wait. You can't see down this guy's throat? OK, look at the picture the picture below.

© Rachata Teyparsit/Shutterstock.com

If all these parts are in working order, you should be able to articulate the phonemes of of most languages spoken today. Phonemes are the smallest individual sounds in language. In the case of sign language, these are called chereme. Phonemes are put together to form words.

When our articulators are not working up to par there can be trouble.

- Placement problems of the tongue produce a lisp.
- A cold, which causes the nasal cavity to fill up makes it difficult to produce nasal sounds.
- Pushing too much sound through the nose causes a nasal whine that is very unpleasant.

Articulation is not uniform across languages.

Khoisan languages. These languages are indigenous to various regions in Africa. They employ a click sound that is made by placing the tongue in specific places in the mouth. The click sound produces a consonant. One of these click languages, Ju'hoan, has 48 click consonants. Because of the addition of click consonants Khoisan languages have more consonants than any other languages. Try learning the click language Xhosa, the native language of Nelson Mandela.

https://youtu.be/31zzMb3U0iY

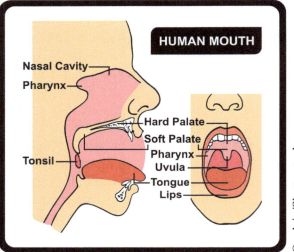

HUMAN MOUTH

Nasal Cavity
Pharynx
Hard Palate
Soft Palate
Pharynx
Uvula
Tongue
Lips
Tonsil

© udaix/Shutterstock.com

© ekler/Shutterstock.com

Pronunciation

Once you learn the sounds of English, you put them together to make words. Pronunciation is the act or result of producing the sounds of speech, including articulation, stress, and intonation, often with reference to some standard (www.dictionary.com). American English has a standard pronunciation for every word. If you want to know what that standard is you can look it up or have Siri pronounce it for you. Since we all have accents, we all deviate from the standard to one degree or another.

© Marijus Auruskevicius/Shutterstock.com

Pronunciation is important. Mispronouncing words means effective communication is in jeopardy. Some things to watch out for.

- Misplaced accent
  - ❏ Syl-LA-ble. Wrong
  - ❏ SYL-la-ble. Right
- Addition of sounds.
  - ❏ Ath-a-lete. Wrong
  - ❏ Ath-lete. Right
- Subtraction of sounds
  - ❏ gover-ment. Wrong
  - ❏ govern-ment. Right
- Transposition of sounds
  - ❏ modren. Wrong
  - ❏ modern. Right

Some commonly mispronounced words.

Word	Commonly Mispronunciation	Standard Pronunciation
Ask	Axe	Ask
Utmost	Up-most	Utmost
Nuclear	Nuk-u-lar	Nu-cle-ar
Similar	Sim-u-lar	Sim-i-ler
Arctic	Art-ic	Arc-tic
Erudite	Air-ee-oo-dite	Air-u-dite

Accents and Dialects

Everyone has an accent. Everyone has a dialect, too.

- An accent is the way you sound, the intonation and music of your voice.
- A dialect incorporates your accent and adds to that the grammar and vocabulary you use.

Your accent is a product of where you have lived, what you heard from your parents, the languages you speak and what language you are speaking at any given time. All language has rhythm and cadence as well as ways of producing sound that are not easily moved from one language to the next.

- English, German, and Spanish roll the "r." American English does not.
- There is no equivalent to the "x" sound in some Asia languages.

One reason it may be difficult to understand your friend whose native language is Arabic, is because the articulation and cadence of spoken Arabic is very different from that of English. While English is being spoken by your friend, it simply doesn't sound like it.

Your accent is part of who you are. You can keep it or change it or change it up depending on where you are. It is up to you. Just remember that your accent may be difficult for others to understand. If you say "earl" when you mean "oil" because you are from Brooklyn, NY, you will have a problem being understood.

Accent Tag is a YouTube channel that lets you hear the same words spoken by people from different part of the English-speaking world.

https://www.youtube.com/results?search_query=accent+tag

What do we learn from listening to Accent Tag? That everybody has an accent, that's what. We also learn that some accents are easier for us to understand than others.

We also learn that we have stereotypes we connect with accents.

- Southerners are slow and stupid.
- Brooklynites are uneducated.
- Upper class British are smart and sophisticated.

Watch this video
https://youtu.be/Kmum-eT4hzM

What do you think? How do you react to this young man? Is he right in his beliefs about his accent?

Enunciation

Enunciation is clear speaking. It's as simple as that. Many of us mumble or speak quickly, or we slur or bunch up our words. All three of those habits prevent effective communication. The goal is to pronounce your words as understandably as possible, to speak at a normal pace and use cadence and rhythm to make yourself understood.

There are six aspects of the voice that combine to make up vocal cues and when used well aid in clear speaking.

© Gino Santa Maria/Shutterstock.com

Volume

Volume is the loudness or softness of your voice. You make the choice about how loudly or softly you will speak. You do this because volume

© Olivier Le Moal /Shutterstock.com

- Expresses emotion—
    - ❏ We often speak louder when we are angry or excited.
    - ❏ Softly when we are sad or content.

- Expresses culture: you are from the loud family.
- Expresses insecurity: we speak softly if we are not sure of ourselves.

Context plays a role in our use of volume. We need to dial it up to 11 when in a big room if we want people in the back to hear us. Intimate conversations require reduced volume if you do not want to be overheard.

Rate

Rate is the speed at which you speak. In average American English we speak at 125–150 words a minute. Anything faster than that can cause comprehension problems. This is not true of all cultures. Many cultures have a rate that is faster and that can be a difficulty especially over the phone.

Rate varies from region to region. The nature of the southern accent slows down speech. People from Northeastern cities speak quickly, in a clipped accent and rapid cadence.

© ktsdesign/Shutterstock.com

What influence the rate of speed at which we speak?

- Nervousness—tension and stress can increase rate.
- Comprehension—we speak slowly to help others understand.
- Excitement—we speak faster the more excited we get.

Pause

Pausing is like punctuation. It lets the listener know that you have come to the end of a thought. It emphasizes those things you believe to be important. If done incorrectly, it can lead to confusion.

© Rawpixel.com/Shutterstock.com

- Example
  - ❏ Eats shoots and leaves
  - ❏ Eats, shoots, and leaves

- Example
  - ❏ Let's eat Grandma.
  - ❏ Let's eat, Grandma

Pitch

Pitch refers to the vibration of the vocal folds that produce the timber of the voice. Meaning that pitch is the variety of "notes" your voice can produce from the very low to the very high.

Think James Earl Jones to Minnie Mouse.

You have control over this. The average voice has a two octave range. You can decide if you wish to sound gruff (low pitches) or irritating (high pitches).

Your voice is an important part of your

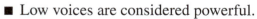
© Orla/Shutterstock.com

communication arsenal. Pitch can convey a variety of positive and negative attributes that will affect your ability to exchange meaning.

- Low voices are considered powerful.
  - ❏ There is a reason James Earl Jones was chosen to voice Darth Vader. His voice is deep and resonant. He sounds menacing.
  - ❏ Imagine Darth Vader with a tenor voice. Can't do it. Not scary enough.

- High voices are considered less powerful.
  - ❏ Luke Skywalker's voice has median pitch. He is supposed to sound young and inexperienced, which because of of that median pitch, he does.
  - ❏ Imagine Luke with Darth Vader's voice. Can't do it. It doesn't work.

And now we will talk about the upward tick that's become so popular? The use of pitch so that every sentence sounds like you are asking a question? This is a recent dialect affectation? Doesn't it make you crazy? Yup.

This use of the upward inflection at the end of every sentence appears to have been brought to us by the California Valley Girl. It is a use of pitch that is generally confined to women but can occasionally be found in young men. It's a problem in search of a solution. Ending each sentence with an upward inflection creates

- An impression of weakness.
- An impression of ignorance.
- An impression of youth.
- An impression of insecurity.

None of these are the impression you might wish to make on others.

Vocal Variety

Vocal variety, intonation, vocal inflections are the names we give to what amounts to the melody of your voice. It is what makes your voice interesting to listen to and what conveys the most to the listener. This is what keeps you from sounding like Data in Star Trek: The Next Generation.

© Yuriy Boyko/Shutterstock.com

Vocal variety combines all of the other aspect of the voice. Its purpose is to convey meaning. Through vocal variety you

- Convey emotion.
- Ask a question.
- Demand an answer.
- Convey interest.

The better able you are to control your voice, the better you will be able to communicate.

Chapter 7

"Sixty percent of all human communication is nonverbal, body language; thirty percent is your tone. So that means that ninety percent of what you're saying ain't coming out of your mouth. Of course she's going to lie to you! She's a nice person."

—*Hitch*

A Discussion of Nonverbal Communication

© ESB Professional/Shutterstock.com

There are a lot of freelance body language experts out there who will tell you that they can explain your behavior by looking at your back teeth. In reality, interpreting nonverbal communication is not that easy. In the first place, nonverbal communication is not just body language. It is a whole raft of behaviors that include gift-giving, how one uses time, touch, clothing, artifacts, and spatial considerations. In fact, nonverbal communication comprises all communication activity that is not language. It is **Communicating Without Words.**

Hitch is right. Most of what we communicate we communicate nonverbally. That is why understanding and controlling our nonverbal communication is so important. That doesn't mean that verbal and nonverbal communication are entirely separate or that verbal communication is unimportant. Here's what we need to know about verbal and nonverbal communication:

POINT/COUNTERPOINT

VERBAL	NONVERBAL
is a single channel phenomenon. Words come at us one at a time. They are sequential.	is a multichannel phenomenon. Nonverbal cues come at you in clusters. They can be overwhelming in their numbers.
has a beginning, a middle, and an end. Again, it is sequential. Whether someone is writing, speaking, emailing, using sign language, the message has a definite beginning, middle, and end.	is continuous (remember you communicate even when sleeping) and it is never ending. That is why it is so hard sometimes to know if a nonverbal cue is part of the message.
is thought out. You think before you write or speak. Sometimes it seems that you don't think before you write or speak, but you do. You make the decision to communicate verbally.	just is. You may think out some of your cues— what you will wear to the party—but much of your nonverbal is unconsciously done. If you ever wondered why people ask you what you are thinking or if you are paying attention it is because you had zoned out without even realizing it.

This little list holds an interesting secret. Notice that the verbal side appears to be conscious and controlled while the nonverbal side seems to be wild and free. So, if you had the choice would you be more likely to believe verbal or nonverbal cues if there was a conflict between them, if the speaker was sending mixed cues? If you said nonverbal you stand with most people. People tend to believe nonverbal cues at a greater rate than verbal and it is because they believe one can lie with words but not with nonverbal.

IMPORTANT CHARACTERISTICS OF NONVERBAL COMMUNICATION

Nonverbal cues reveal relationship status

This means that nonverbal cues have social functions. Monitoring and carefully choosing your nonverbal cues helps others know what kind of relationships you have and how they are to approach you.

Nonverbal cues work in a variety of ways to alert others to your relational status:

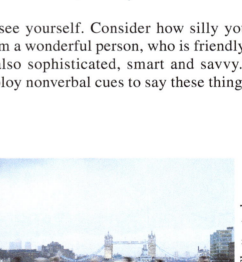

© photomak/Shutterstock.com

- They work to help us build and maintain relationships with people.
- They alert people to your relational status—think Facebook.
- They serve to keep people at a distance or bring them close.
- Socially, nonverbal can convey emotions that we may be unable or unwilling to express.
  - ❏ Nonverbal is much better suited to conveying attitudes and feelings than ideas. Save the ideas for verbal communication.
  - ❏ Even if someone is speaking a language we don't understand, we may be able to understand how that person is feeling.
- You want people to see you in the same way you see yourself. Consider how silly you would sound to someone if you met and said "Hi! I am a wonderful person, who is friendly, thoughtful, caring and good with children. I am also sophisticated, smart and savvy." You'd probably run away from that person. You employ nonverbal cues to say these things instead.

Nonverbal cues never stop

We may not be speaking but our nonverbal cues are saying things.

This does not mean that we are always aware of the nonverbal cues we send or that people will accurately interpret our nonverbal cues, but it does mean that we are sending messages continually.

The key for effective communication is to figure out which nonverbal cues relate to the message and need attention and which you can ignore.

© Mark Yuill/Shutterstock.com

Nonverbal cues are not easily understood

If we read a lot of books on nonverbal cues we get the idea that all nonverbal cues mean the same thing. They don't.

Have you ever wondered why there is so much confusion about how men and women should deal with one another in a business setting? Well, this is the reason. The nonverbal cues men and women use in a social setting are not appropriate in the business yet the social cues are often imported into the business setting. Hence, confusion abounds. Culture plays a role here as well.

Nonverbal behaviors can have multiple meanings.

❏ A yawn does not always mean you are bored.
❏ Crossed arms does not always mean you are angry.
❏ Tears don't always mean you are sad.

Nonverbal cues are culturally specific

We learn much of our nonverbal behaviors in childhood. Our parents and others pass these on to us.

As we grow up in a cultural group we adopt the nonverbal cues of that group. This is true of co-cultures which exist in the wider society.

Nonverbal cues are more concrete than abstract

This seems to fly in the face of what you just read above. However, objects and actions are less abstract than words. They also are able to generate emotions.

If you hit someone that person is fairly certain what you mean by that. Consequently, you are likely to receive the same in return. If someone hugs you that cue is also obvious.

Nonverbal cues must be in sync with verbal cues

When verbal and nonverbal cues match you are much more likely to interpret the message correctly. When they don't match meaning is lost.

Nonverbal and verbal should work together to make a complete effective message.

Here are some ways to make that happen:

© PhotoMediaGroup/Shutterstock.com

- Use nonverbal to accent a verbal cue. You grab your hair in frustration while you swear at the blue screen of death. The table for emphasis.
- Use nonverbal to enhance or show your underlying feelings. You smile or laugh to show a story is funny.
- Use nonverbal to mean the opposite of what you say. You wink to show you are kidding.
- Use nonverbal to control the communication situation. Your You put your fingers to your lips in the theater to keep your friend from talking.
- Use nonverbal to repeat the message. You wave good bye and you say, "Good bye."
  - ❏ And if you don't feel like saying "good bye," nonverbal can do the job for you by the simple wave gesture. (Wertheim, 2017)

INFLUENCES ON NONVERBAL CUES

Our nonverbal cues are influenced by a wide variety of factors. We can begin to analyze our nonverbal skill-set by doing an inventory of what influences are at play in our choices.

Attitudes about People

How we view others will influence our nonverbal cues.

If you like someone you are likely to try to be on time for that person.

If you want to show someone you care you will buy a nice gift.

If you want to show the the person your friend set you up with you are not interested, you dress down for the first date.

© Stuart Miles/Shutterstock.com

Authority Rank and Status

Our nonverbal cues are influenced by how we view authority in our relationships.

You stand for the elderly or the boss or somebody you want to impress.

You have a spiffy office with windows to show you are the boss.

Your uniform indicates your rank.

© Ruslan Grechka /Shutterstock.com

Context/Setting

The context alerts us to appropriate nonverbal cues. You will assess the context and decide what works nonverbally and what is expected. It is up to you to decide if you are going to adhere to them.

- No white dresses at a wedding unless you are the bride (in America).
- You paint your face with the colors of your team.
- You must cover your tattoos at your workplace.

© fstockfoto/Shutterstock.com

Culture

This may be the strongest influence as cultural nonverbal cues are impressed on us at a very early age.

- Dress codes
- Personal space cues
- Gestures
- Food
- Touch
- Colors

© Juliya Shangarey/Shutterstock.com

Cultures also differ in how they assess the importance of nonverbal cues. Cultures are on a continuum of high context to low context in their assessments of nonverbal communication. We saw this earlier but should review the differences between high and low context cultures.

- High Context Cultures
  - ❏ Generally, more collectivist in nature
  - ❏ Nonverbal is very important
  - ❏ Personal relationships are important
  - ❏ Former interactions important

- Low Context Cultures
  - ❏ Generally, more individualistic in nature
  - ❏ Explicit communication
  - ❏ Verbal is more important
  - ❏ Written contracts

Impression Management

How you choose to present yourself in public also influences your nonverbal.

Presenting as a hip, sophisticated person has you dressing and behaving in a way that highlights these characteristics.

Presenting as an "I don't care what people think" person has you dressing and behaving in a way that highlights that.

© Nejron Photo/Shutterstock.com

Self-Concept

Who we are will affect our nonverbal communication.

Outgoing people tend to wear bright colors, sit close to people, gesture, and perhaps even touch others.

Shy people do not do these things. Their nonverbal choices allow them to recede into the background.

These influences work together. Influences on nonverbal cues cannot be looked at in isolation. We are back to what we discussed in Chapter 2. You need to analyze the communication situation, plug in the model's components and decide how you will employ nonverbal communication in that setting.

© WAYHOME studio/Shutterstock.com

All this is to say that nonverbal communication is not a precise science. People who study nonverbal can become better at interpreting it, but there is no precise, 100% accurate way of understanding another's nonverbal communication—*Lie to Me* and *Criminal Minds,* notwithstanding.

Look at this clip from the TV show Criminal Minds.
https://youtu.be/dmDNRq82rt8

What does this clip tell you? What is Agent Hotchner observing? How many nonverbal cues does he mark as he takes down the lawyer? Can this happen in real life?

KINESICS, PROXEMICS, AND HAPTICS, OH MY!

Nonverbal cues are many and varied. Google "categories of nonverbal communication" and you will find list after list of suggestions of what constitutes a nonverbal cue. That Google search should tell you that nonverbal communication is not simply "body language" which is the first answer most people give when asked to define nonverbal. Nonverbal is so much more than gestures and facial expressions.

© Kheng Guan Toh/Shutterstock.com

If you think time, gift-giving, and food are not nonverbal cues then you are in for a surprise. Nonverbal includes all that and more. Obviously then, what is discussed below is all there is not to know. The categories chosen for this textbook are the ones that we need the most practice recognizing and and there is always more to learn.

We start with:

PHYSICAL NONVERBAL CUES

Body Shape and Weight or Physical Features

- The first nonverbal cue people receive from you is your physical appearance.
    - Height
    - Weight
    - Ethnicity
    - Gender

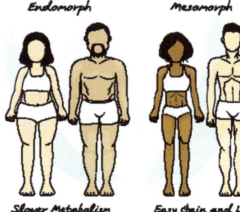
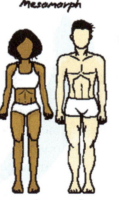
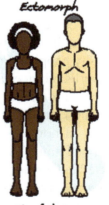

© Kade Sudkamon/Shutterstock.com

People begin to size you up immediately based on how they perceive you look. We are not talking clothing and artifacts here. We are talking about your physical characteristics.

- Some physical characteristics can be changed. Examples are:
    - Eye color
    - Hair color
    - Nose
    - Lips

- Some are completely out of your control.
    - You can't do anything about how tall you are, although women wear heels and men wear lifts to make themselves appear taller.

❑ The size of your hands and feet are not in your control.
❑ Some people seem not to be able to lose or gain weight
- Your body shape puts you into one of three categories, each with its own unfortunate stereotype. These three types are:

The Ectomorph: The thin, maybe tall, small shoulders and small muscles type

And here are some famous ectomorphs. Notice that being an ectomorph does not mean you are frail or weak. There are athletes and action stars and martial artists in this group. You can see that the stereotype does not hold.

Famous Ectomorphs:
http://elitheillusionist.wixsite.com/ectomorphzone/celebrities-who-are-ectomorphs

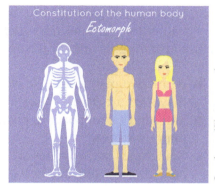

The Mesomorph: The mesomorph has wide shoulders and a small waist. This works out to an hour glass figure for women and the triangle shape for men.

Contrary to popular stereotype such people are not stupid. Arnold Schwarzenegger, for example, made huge amounts of money in the real estate market in California.

Famous Mesomorphs:
http://www.superskinnyme.com/mesomorph-body-type.html
https://www.pinterest.com/dream_it/mesomorph-body-type/

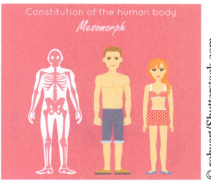

The Endomorph: On the plump side. Can be muscular and does have trouble losing and keeping weight off.

Contrary to popular opinion, I mean look at these people, they are very attractive and do not look like that lack self-control.

Famous Endomorphs:
http://www.superskinnyme.com/endomorph-body-type.html
https://www.pinterest.com/dream_it/endomorph-body-type/

What does this all mean?
- You perceive yourself as being one of these and behave in a way that reinforces your beliefs about how a person with that body type should be.

- Your feelings about your body type will be conveyed to those around you through your non-verbal cues.
  - ❏ If you are comfortable with your body type that will show.
  - ❏ If you are not comfortable with it that will show.
- You assess every aspect of your personal appearance and decide if you like it. You know that there are things about you that you don't like. You might try to do something about that: change hair color, get your nose fixed, and do body building.

Some interesting information here:

- Attractive people—those whom society thinks are attractive or who give the impression that they are attractive—make more money.
- Tall men (a supposedly positive physical trait in men) make on average 12% more income than short men.
- Sometimes attractiveness is a liability. The nonverbal cue may say "this person is not smart" or encourage jealousy or belief that the person did not get a job on merit but because of the looks.

BODY MOVEMENTS

© Syda Productions /Shutterstock.com

Kinesics is the term we use to describe the act of interpreting body movements as nonverbal messages. While you might conclude that this practice refers to gestures and eye contact in reality there is more to it than that. Below is a list of body movements that need interpretation if meaning is to be exchanged.

Emblems

These always have a direct verbal translation. They are used to replace verbal communication.

© leolintang/Shutterstock.com

- A wave of the hand.
- A thumbs up.
- An "L" on the forehead for "loser."
- A "W" for whatever.

The meaning of a particular gesture changes from culture to culture. It is important to know what gestures mean before you go using them and find yourself in trouble.

Illustrators

These gestures are used when you think your words do not convey enough information. You use your body to "paint a picture" for your listener.

Essentially, these body movements reinforce your message. Or you can define this type of body movement as "talking with your hands."

But as you can see from the picture to your left, illustrators can and do employ the entire body.

© Mert Toker/Shutterstock.com

Affect Displays

These body movements convey emotions. And as with illustrators they can use the entire body to do so.

Some people are more demonstrative than others. You know who you are. You jump up and down. You high five. You fist pump. All those body movements are affect displays.

© stockyimages/Shutterstock.com

Regulators

You were introduced to this type of communication earlier when you read about how nonverbal works. These cues control communication.

- Raised hands in a classroom.
- A head nod to indicate it is your time to speak.
- Your mom grabbing your arm to keep you from running out into the street.

© HBRH/Shutterstock.com

Adaptors 1

Cues that meet a personal need.

Scratching an itch or belching fall into this category.

You are more likely to perform these cues in private and try to hide them in public.

© Augustino/Shutterstock.com

Adaptors 2

They are objects that are manipulated for a purpose.

- Using a pen as a pointer.
- Gesturing with your eye glasses.
- Using eye glasses to make yourself appear more scholarly.

© leungchopan/Shutterstock.com

Facial Expressions

Your face is the most expressive part of your body.

Research tells us that the face suggests 10 basic classes of meaning: happiness, surprise, fear, anger, sadness, disgust, contempt, interest, bewilderment, and determination.

Unsurprisingly, your face can communicate more than one of these at a time. That is why it is sometimes hard to read a person's face.

We pay more attention to the face than to any other nonverbal cue. Again, this is unsurprising because the face is so expressive. Also, it is difficult, but not impossible, to keep our emotions off our faces. No one has to tell you how hard it is to keep from crying.

© Kotin/Shutterstock.com

Because the face is so expressive and can pass through various emotions very quickly, it is not easy to decode these nonverbal cues. Also,

- Not everyone conveys emotions in the same way.
- Some people are better at controlling their faces.
- Some people are better at decoding these cues than others.

Eye Contact

Eye contact is a culturally specific non-verbal cue. And while this is true of every nonverbal cue, people seem to place special importance on eye contact in this regard.

Some cultures find direct eye contact disrespectful. In America, we generally require eye contact to show respect and truthfulness.

Know your culture before employing this cue.

You use eye contact as a nonverbal cue for specific reasons

© Knot P. Saengma/Shutterstock.com

- For feedback. You look at the speaker or listener to see if this person is receiving the message or so you can better understand the message.
- To regulate communication. By making eye contact you tell the other it is time to speak.
- As a relationship indicator.
  - ❏ Eye contact can be used to show who is superior.
    - ● Superiors look you in the eye.
    - ● You look away.
  - ❏ Who is dominant?
  - ❏ Whether you like or don't like someone.
- To shorten the distance between two points. Catching someone's eye across a crowded room psychologically lessens the distance between you.
- To replace verbal.
  - ❏ Your mother gives you "the look." You know what that means.
  - ❏ You make eye contact with someone at a party to say, "Let's go."
- To avoid unpleasantness.
  - ❏ You might look away from a mother arguing with her child in a store believing that this offers them a measure of privacy.
  - ❏ You close your eyes to listen to music.
  - ❏ You close your eyes at the movies at really scary parts.

CLOTHING

© Inspiring/Shutterstock.com

Why do you wear clothes? Don't laugh. It's a serious question. Make a list:

1)
2)
3)
4)
5)

Clothing is not worn simply because of social convention or the weather. Clothing is worn to communicate. What does clothing communicate? Make another list:

1)
2)
3)
4)
5)

Some examples of what clothing communicate:

- Economic status
  - ❏ High-end fabrics
  - ❏ High-end labels
- Education
  - ❏ Academic regalia (robes and hats differ by degree attained)
  - ❏ Ballet attire
- Group membership
  - ❏ Military
  - ❏ Sports team

Clothing communicates because it is **symbolic.** It says something about

- who you are;
- what you think and feel about yourself;
- the place you wish to be in society;
- what you think about your society and culture.

Clothing is not neutral. What you wear sends messages to those around you. You might not think that you are sending a message, but you are.

- And people will judge you for it.
- When someone doesn't know you the only clue they have is your nonverbal.
- If your nonverbal makes them uncomfortable for whatever reason you will have trouble communicating.

Here is a good article on a new field of study called "enclothed cognition." Enclothed cognition suggests that we think differently depending on how we are dressed. If true, think about how clothing will affect your ability to get a job or be taken seriously by a possible romantic partner. http://www.nytimes.com/2012/04/03/science/clothes-and-self-perception.html

CLOTHING BY DEFINITION

Which one of these women is the salesperson and which the customer? Why did you make your decision? What did you focus on to make that decision? What was it about their clothing that made you think one was the salesperson and one the customer?

Maybe we should all wear uniforms. The Western world used to run like that. People wore clothing that indicated to those around them what they did for a living. Were you to walk down a London street with Sherlock Holmes, you like he, would be able to pick out the nanny, the messenger boy, the tradesman, the nurse, and the clergy simply by observing what they were wearing.

Each one of the people in the photo is wearing a uniform. It may not look like it at first glance because we often think of uniforms like this:

But look closely again at the first picture. Now list what you think this person does, based on the clothing choices this person has made.

Ask yourself these questions:

- What is the purpose of a uniform?
- Why are they worn?
- What does the uniform say to you?

Uniforms generate an aura of authority and respect. Uniforms also tell people you are part of a group. They inhibit individuality. They circumscribe behavior. They also say, "This person means business."

McDonald's Corporation just made a change to their uniforms. The decision was made apparently to help their employees "fit in" better with the world when going to and from work. The old brightly colored uniforms screamed MCDONALD'S and seemed to make employees uncomfortable in when picking up kids from daycare or stopping in at the local bar after work. What do you think?

http://www.cnbc.com/2017/04/25/mcdonalds-uniforms-look-like-evil-star-wars-employees-say-tweeters.html

UNIFORMS IN PUBLIC SCHOOLS LET'S DEBATE

Should public schools require uniforms for their students?

Yes They Should	No They Shouldn't
1.	1.
2.	2.
3.	3.

Should public schools require uniforms for their teachers?

Yes They Should	No They Shouldn't
1.	1.
2.	2.
3.	3.

You define yourself for people by how you dress

By how you dress, you define yourself as a member of a

- cultural group;
- social group;
- profession;
- even your age.

© Milosz Maslanka/Shutterstock.com

Emotional state

You give clues as to your emotional state by how you dress. You have two choices here:

- Bright colors because you feel happy and confident.
- Clean, well-fitting clothes show confidence.

Dress down because you feel down or dress up because you feel up.

Overdressing may indicate anxiety about a situation. Dressing down may show that you don't care.

© kurhan/Shutterstock.com

Fashion says me too. Style says only me

You define yourself as being set apart or as wanting to be one of the crowd.

This woman is part of the steampunk movement. She is certainly set apart from the everyday.

There is a couple in London who are trying to live like Victorians. They go out every day dressed in Victorian era clothing. That type of dress might not look so odd in London, but might raise some eyebrows in Muncie, Indiana.

© Kiselev Andrey Valerevich/Shutterstock.com

ARTIFACTS

Now we come to artifacts. Artifacts are objects we use to communicate the following:

■ Personality
■ Group membership
■ Ethnicity
■ Heritage
■ Politics
■ Religion

And any other thing you can think of.
     Artifacts can be worn.

© Tepikina Nastya/Shutterstock.com

Hairstyles

© Daniel M Ernst/Shutterstock.com

Facial Hair

©pixelheadphoto digitalskillet /Shutterstock.com

Cosmetics

© photoagent/Shutterstock.com

Tattoos

© FXQuadro/Shutterstock.com

Jewelry

© Lutsenko_Oleksandr/Shutterstock.com

© Natalia Davidovich/Shutterstock.com

Piercings

These pictures show a good deal of variety across cultures and lifestyles. Notice that these artifacts are all choices the individual makes.

BEARDS AND WHAT THEY CONVEY

© Volodymyr Tverdokhlib/Shutterstock.com

© Luis Molinero/Shutterstock.com

Is this what you consider a true beard? Too small? Too big?

Which do you like best?

What does each say to you?

ARTIFACTS CAN BE ENVIRONMENTAL

Cars

© Matyas Rehak/Shutterstock.com

Houses

© Kakabadze George/Shutterstock.com

Interior Design

© ImageFlow/Shutterstock.com

Landscaping

© photowind/Shutterstock.com

Artifacts can be used to send specific messages like:

I am married

© Myronovych/Shutterstock.com

I am a citizen of Australia

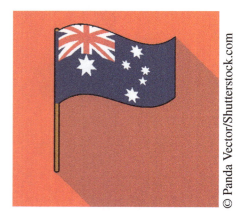

© Panda Vector/Shutterstock.com

I am a Mason

© Carnegie42/Shutterstock.com

I am religious

© wajedram/Shutterstock.com

Artifacts are also ambiguous which means the message is not always clear. Join in a discussion of artifacts by answering the questions above the photos and sharing your answers.

Am I whimsical or do I have bad taste?

© Anton Watman/Shutterstock.com

Am I a Star Wars fan or did my boss make me do this?

© Grzegorz Czapski/Shutterstock.com

Am I making a statement about how I feel or am I just having fun?

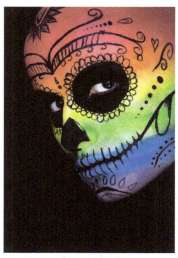

© Lena Bukovsky/Shutterstock.com

Artifacts send culturally specific messages.

A woman of the Kayan people of Myanmar

© Nattawut Jaroenchai/Shutterstock.com

Sikh man praying at the Golden Temple at Amritsar

© Phuong D. Nguyen/Shutterstock.com

Pirate

© Kazanovskyi Andrii/Shutterstock.com

HAPTICS TOUCHING BEHAVIOR

Haptics is the study of touching behavior. Your own experience of touching others and being touched tells you that touching behavior means different things at different times and in different places. Unsurprisingly this is because of the influences on touching behavior:

© Rawpixel.com/Shutterstock.com

- Context—social or business.
- Relationship—acquaintance, role, friend, or intimate.
- Culture—high context or low context.
- Attitudes about people—like or don't like.
- Personality—outgoing or shy.

Meaning of Touch

Touch conveys four different categories of meaning. Here they are:

Positive or Negative Affect Display

Show support, appreciation, and affection like this soccer team or show dislike, enmity, and hostility like these two.

Play Display

- Lightens interaction.
- Shows you are having fun.
- Encourages others not to take you seriously at this point.
- Shows you want to relax. Do you like being tickled? Is tickling in fact play display or could it fall into the next category?

Control or Status Display

- Used to direct behaviors and attitudes.
- Can communicate dominance.
- Higher status person can initiate touch, proving dominance.

© WDnet Creation/Shutterstock.com

Ritual Display

These are handshakes, hugs, and kisses that indicate greeting or departure.

Cultures develop these as you see from this photograph of novice Buddhist monks greeting each other. Japanese bowing behavior, which is quite complicated, is another.

You develop these with your family and friends. Do you have a secret handshake?

© Tanakorn Pussawong/Shutterstock.com

THE GREAT DEBATE: TO SPANK OR NOT TO SPANK

Take 10 minutes to research on your electronic device your position on spanking a child as a form of discipline. Using the blank space below and outline three arguments in favor of your position. You will have five minutes to present that position.

© Rob Wilson/Shutterstock.com

TYPES OF TOUCH

Touching behavior is influenced by context. A good communicator will assess the context before engaging in any touching behavior. Knowing what is acceptable and what is not in any given context is important if you wish to exchange meaning. Touching behavior is open to disastrous misinterpretation. Here is what you need to know:

Professional Touch. This takes place between people when they are in a business or professional context. Handshakes are a classic example.

Professional touch includes a doctor's examination and a dentist putting fingers in a patient's mouth. This type of personal touch is allowed because the nature of the relationship makes such touching impersonal and safe.

THIS IS NOT AN ACCEPTABLE TOUCH IN A PROFESSIONAL SETTING:

Social Touch. This is what you do at parties, when you meet on the street, etc. Handshakes again. Hugs and kisses.

Look at this picture. Its caption indicates that this is a business situation. But notice the handshake. The woman's hand is positioned in a way that indicates, in American etiquette, a social occasion. For a business situation the woman's hand should be in the same position as the mans, straight and parallel to the hand to be shaken. What does the woman's hand position say to the man? If he knows this etiquette rule? If he doesn't? Does this hand position indicate strength to you?

Friendship Touch. This is between friends. Hugs, kisses, arms around waist or shoulders, sitting on laps, etc. Stuffing yourself and 25 of your closest friends into your Prius.

The degree of friendship you have with another will influence this type of touch. The closer you are as friends that more you touch. For example, you sit thigh to thigh and knee to knee on a couch rather than separating yourselves using the cushions as a boundary.

Intimate Touch. Includes all friendship touch plus all those things you are thinking. On this level, all touching behavior is more intense.

The hug between this father and his son who has Down Syndrome is intimate.

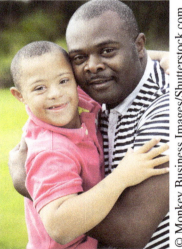

Touching behavior is another culture-specific nonverbal cue. Touching behavior differs from culture to culture. Be aware and learn. In some cultures, it is inappropriate for men and women to touch when out in public. Public displays of affection are permitted in some places and not in others.

What is your opinion of public displays of affection? Where and what?

List the behaviors you think are appropriate for romantic couples in these public spaces.

College hallway:

Coffee Shop:

Public Street:

PROXEMICS SPATIAL CUES

Spatial cues are divided into two categories, environment and territoriality.

- Environment consists of
  - Physical space like the outdoors, buildings, car, and neighborhood and
  - How we manipulate these spaces to make them our own.
- Territoriality consists of
  - Boundaries you set up to protect yourself.
  - Your personal safe space or your personal bubble. Your bubble relates to the accepted physical distances of your culture. In America, it looks like this:
    - Intimate distance. 0–18 inches. Low voice. Touching.
    - Personal. 18 inches to 4 feet. Can still hold confidential conversation. Parties, classroom, and work. If you engage in this you probably know the person well.
    - Social distance. 4–12 feet. Casual. Can also include parties, as well as work or the classroom.
    - Public distance. 12 feet and up. This is public speaking distance.

As with every aspect of communication both the environment and territoriality are influenced by many factors. Let's start with the following.

INFLUENCES ON ENVIRONMENT

Age

One look at the photograph tells you that this room is for children. Even if there were no children in the room you could not fail to see this room as a kid's space.

Feminine or Masculine

You design a space for yourself that falls along a feminine/masculine continuum. Look at the photographs. Which is the feminine room and which is the masculine? Why did you make the decision you made?

Cultural or Ethnic Background

Not all Mongolian yurts are the same. Color, size, and entrance door are individualized to the owner's liking.

Context or Setting

What room is the center of your house? Why?

Kitchens are often considered the center of the home. They are designed for comfort and ease of communication. They are informal.

Living rooms are more formal. Communication changes from kitchen to living room.

© Monkey Business Images /Shutterstock.com

Physical Characteristics

Who we are physically influences the environments we set up for ourselves. Houses designed for people with limited abilities are different than those designed for people without those limitations. Doors are wider, countertops are lower, and bathrooms are accessible.

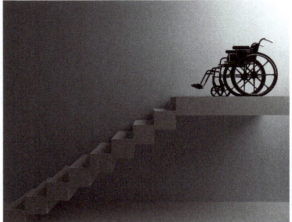

© goa novi/Shutterstock.com

Status

People alert you to their status by the houses in which they live, the cars they drive, and the number of windows in their offices.

And by the stables they own. The building to your left is a stable for horses. Wouldn't you love to see the house?

© Kiev. Victor/Shutterstock.com

Attitudes and Emotions

If you want to alert people to your desire to be alone, if you are a misanthrope, if you just don't want to be around people, you can convey that attitude by where you live.

© Vladimir Mijailovic /Shutterstock.com

ENVIRONMENT: THE PHYSICAL SETTING

Studies show that people can fairly accurately interpret the personality of homeowners by looking at how the house is decorated. Our physical environment tells others about ourselves. People make judgments about us based on what they see of our physical environments. Our houses, our cars, our neighborhoods, our offices, and our dorm rooms.

Architects design spaces that shape interactions within a building's environment. After that it is up to us to make these places our own. We try to manipulate the spaces around us to fit our perceptions of ourselves.

© angkrit/Shutterstock.com

- Formal or informal.
- Classic or modern.
- Sophisticated or down home.

You cannot control permanent structures like the building we are in right now. Would you choose to go to class here, if you had a choice of buildings? Maybe. Maybe not.

What's This?

© Atlaspix/Shutterstock.com

What's This?

Yes, they are both schools. One looks more like a classic school. One looks modern and therefore it's harder to tell that it is a school. It might be anything. How would this environment affect your communication within it?

© Thomason Photography /Shutterstock.com

INFLUENCES ON ENVIRONMENT AND TERRITORIALITY

Age

© Rawpixel.com/Shutterstock.com

We invade the spaces of the elderly and small children without a thought. Why?

You can tell, just by looking which bedrooms in a home belong to the children and which to the adults.

Can parents invade the territory of their children? Can a parent search a child's room? Does that room "belong" to the child?

Sex

Women stand closer to one another than men do. Opposite sex duos stand further apart.

© Rawpixel.com/Shutterstock.com

Cultural or Ethnic Background

Your sense of space, how close you let strangers stand to you for example, is influenced by your culture.

The people in the photograph are sleeping in a train station as they wait for the train to come in. In Varanasi, India where this picture was taken being this close to strangers is not unusual.

People in the United States have a much bigger personal bubble.

The social roles of men and women are at play here as well. There are cultures where women must walk behind men. Prince Phillip on the other hand is required to walk behind his wife, the Queen of England.

Topic or Subject Matter

You stand or sit closer when discussing personal matters.

This influence seems to be dissipating with the use of cell phones. When was the last time you heard a very private matter being discussed via cell phone as you were standing on line at the movies? Did you listen or did you try to put psychological distance between you and the information you didn't want to hear?

Impersonal matters can be shouted across the street.

Setting or Context

Interpersonal communication in a public area requires you to shorten the distance between you.

These young women have pulled their chairs closer together and one is leaning on the table. These things are necessary to be heard. You may not like it because you are too close, but you can't communicate if you don't shorten the distance.

Physical Characteristics

As you get older your personal bubble by necessity must shrink. You are in need of more help and that requires closer contact with people.

© Photographyee.eu /Shutterstock.com

Attitudes and Emotions

How you feel about the topic and the person affects the space at which you communicate. The less you like someone the bigger your personal space.

If you are unhappy you may keep people at a distance.

© Balazs Kovacs Images/Shutterstock.com

Status

People of equal status generally maintain much shorter distances between themselves while conversing.

High status people seem to be able to invade the territory of low status people, but the opposite is unthinkable—the boss can barge into your office at any time, but you can't do the same to your boss.

© Mikael Damkier/Shutterstock.com

TERRITORIALITY

You will stake out territories for yourselves in the environments in which you find yourself. These environments come in three flavors: primary, secondary, and public territory.

- Primary Territory: Your personal space. It consists of
    - Your personal belongings
    - Your house
    - Your bedroom
    - Your specific seat at the table or in the family room
- Secondary Territory:
    - Your favorite place to eat
    - Your favorite bar
    - Your seat in class

- Public Territory: Belongs to everyone, but you think of it as yours:
  - ❑ Your town
  - ❑ Your neighborhood
  - ❑ Your jogging trails

You are not happy when your territory is invaded. Why is that? Well, there is a controversy as to whether this trait is nature or nurture. It probably doesn't matter which it is. People are territorial and want to defend their territories.

You will set up your territories in ways that express who you are. No two offices are the same, for example. You may even find classrooms set up differently depending on who is teaching a given class and the subject matter of that class.

Every semester is different. You have a new set of classes and new instructors. Yet you behave the same way as the first day of every class. You enter the classroom and choose a seat. Then you begin to establish your territory.

- You sit in the back row with your books on a chair next to you.
- You sit in the front row, dead center with your books tucked under your seat.
- You sit right next to the door, laptop on the desk and a clear shot to be the first out of the room.

These seats become "yours" for the rest of the semester. You may have witnessed or been part of the drama of someone taking "another's seat" in a classroom. Territories are important to us. And they appear to be important to your success in college.

- The students sitting in the front rows of a high-enrollment introductory physics class (Physics 1010, Physics of Everyday Life) received better grades than students in the back—even though seats were randomly assigned at the beginning of the course (Kalinowski and Tapper 2007).
- Studies show that students who sit in front do better than those who sit in the middle or in the back.
- Studies also show that the very worst place to sit is in the middle of the room.

The same thing seems to be true with parking spaces. Studies show that you will take more time leaving a parking space if someone is waiting for it. It's yours after all and you don't want to give it up.

You Are Sitting in My Seat

Answer the following as they relate to this classroom:

I would rather sit in the	FRONT	MIDDLE	BACK
I want to sit next to people	YES	NO	DON'T CARE
I want to sit near the door	YES	NO	DON'T CARE
I want to sit near the window	YES	NO	DON'T CARE

I try to expand my territory by doing the following: (List as many things as you wish.)

Where you live is a territory you have staked out for yourself. Your choice includes:

- Country
- State
- City, suburb, town village
- Rural
- Neighborhood

Once this is decided you go on to your next choice

- Rent
  - ❏ Apartment building
  - ❏ Old house
  - ❏ Something more funky
- Own
  - ❏ Big or little
  - ❏ New construction or old
  - ❏ Style (modern, Victorian, cottage)

What does your choice say about you? What do you want it to say?

City people view themselves differently than country people view themselves. Billy Joel's "Uptown Girl" and John Denver's "Thank God I'm a country boy" are indicators of cultural perceptions of the town/country mindset. Such territory designations explain a lot about how people perceive themselves, especially in terms of values.

Which of these is more appealing to you?

Montpelier, VT

Or

New York City, NY

Explain your answer.

Once we choose our territories we then do our very best to defend them. This is how we do it according to Jennifer Tylee (2011):

BARRIERS

Yes, we set up barriers to keep people away. These barriers can be both physical and psychological.

Central Markers: items you place in the territory to reserve this territory for yourself. Book bags on tables and chairs.

Boundary Markers: divides your territory from another's.
Example would be the bar that divides groceries on the conveyor belt; fixed arms on seats in movie theaters.

Earmarkers: marks that clearly indicate that something is yours.

- Monograms
- Your name on your clothes
- Tattoos

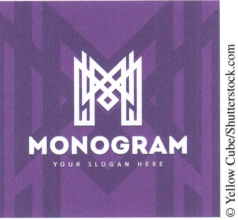

OTHER TYPES OF NONVERBAL CUES

Now comes a group of nonverbal cues that we don't often think about, but are nonetheless important. This group includes color, smell, time, and gift-giving.

Color

This is a fascinating nonverbal cue as it has the following aspects to it:

- Psychological
- Cultural
- Emotional

You react to colors. Some you like, some you don't. Color means something to you that it may not mean to others.

In America what are we talking about here? How do we view color and its meaning?

- Red—passion and excitement
- White—purity
- Black—sophistication
- Blue—calm, serene, or sadness
- Green—health, good luck, and inexperience
- Yellow—joy, happiness, and betrayal
- Purple—royalty, passion, and religiosity

Color is used to define events, people, and states of being:

- Valentine's Day is red, red, red.
- Brides wear white.
- Black is for mourning.
- Politically: left is blue, right is red.

Color can influence moods.

- Red helps us generate excitement.
- Blue helps us be soothed and comforted.
- Yellow helps us be cheerful and jovial.

Color is used to conform or not conform to cultural norms.

- You paint your house a shocking pink.
- You wear white to a wedding when you are not the bride.
- Your tuxedo is powder blue.

As with all things the use of color as a nonverbal cue is culturally specific. Here are some examples:

- Wedding dresses. China and India, red. Morocco, yellow.
- Mourning: China, white. Egypt, yellow. Korea, blue.
- Gender: Japan, pink is a man's color. Nepalese women wear more colorful clothing than men.

Use the following colors in a sentence

These color names have meaning beyond expressing the color you prefer. Use each in a sentence.
Red

Green

Yellow

Why did you answer the way you did?

Smell

Smell is a powerful nonverbal cue. You know this from your own experiences. Just get a whiff of that pepperoni pizza and you start craving it.

You are an individual and will have your own unique reaction to smells. Some you like and some you don't.

Some things you can't smell but others you can. In other words, some people's noses are more sensitive than others. And of course, you can lose your sense of smell completely. Once that happens a whole category of nonverbal cues is closed to you. Then your friends can play tricks on you by making you drink stuff you don't like, but you don't realize it because once you lose your sense of smell you lose your sense of taste.

Below you will find a variety of different ways smells send messages

© LightField Studios /Shutterstock.com

Attraction

- We use smells that will attract others to us.
- Foods are considered pleasing or not depending on how they smell.

© alphaspirit/Shutterstock.com

Traits

Apparently, research shows that smell conveys personality traits.

- Cedar, orange, lime, cinnamon, and peppermint signal intelligence.
- Vanilla, jasmine, and lemongrass invoke kindness.
- Pepper, marjoram, basil, and tangerine tell others you are humorous and playful.
- Orange, sandalwood, and frankincense imply safety.

© Keith Bell/Shutterstock.com

Taste

Your taste buds are affected by your sense of smell. If your nose is blocked you can't taste food. That means you can eat things you typically don't like because you can't taste them.

Memory

Smell works as a memory trigger. You know what your Granma's house smelled like. Every time you encounter that smell you are immediately brought back to your Granma's.

- Places you have been.
- People you have known.

This is why widowed people keep the clothing of a deceased spouse.

Cultural Differences

How you react to odors and what you consider appropriate are culturally determined.

In America, we like to cover up the natural smell of the body.

- Europeans bathe less frequently than Americans.
- Arab cultures prefer the natural smell of the body.
- Asians bathe more frequently than Americans who bathe more frequently than Europeans.

The above photograph depicts a Japanese bathhouse. Bathing in Japan, for men, is a public undertaking. It is an important and necessary ritual.

Japanese bathing customs require a number of implements which you can see by the pictures to the right. These nonverbal cues tell you how important cleanliness is to the Japanese.

© Steinar/Shutterstock.com

Emotional Trigger

Smell triggers feelings in us.

Real estate agents have you bake bread, cookies, or pies when people are coming to look at your house so your house smells "like a home."

Air fresheners, spa oils, and bubble bath are all given odors that evoke an emotional response from you.

© g-stockstudio/Shutterstock.com

Identification

You know where you are by how it smells, even if you are blindfolded.

The smell of a product does not affect its ability to perform, but you identify certain smells with clean (pine, lemon) and are more likely to buy them.

© Africa Studio/Shutterstock.com

CHRONEMICS

TIME AND HOW YOU USE IT

© Alexey Wraith/Shutterstock.com

How you organize and react to time is a nonverbal cue. People react to and are aware of time based on all the factors we have discussed above, but most specifically culture. There are vast differences between cultures in how they view time and we need to be aware of that.

The culture continuum runs from monochromic to polychromic.

- Monochronic: Time is valuable.
  - ❑ Expected to be prompt.
  - ❑ There is an appropriate time and place for everything.
  - ❑ Values orderliness.
  - ❑ Values finishing work on time.
  - ❑ Example: United States, Germany.
- Polychronic: Time is multidimensional. Therefore, time is not valuable.
  - ❑ Things happen together. There is no sense of a step-by-step process.
  - ❑ Not necessary to be on time, to start and end at a specific time.
  - ❑ Interruptions are expected and not considered rude.
  - ❑ Examples: India, Brazil.

You can see how these cultural expectations can cause communication breakdowns. You, an American wait and wait for your friend, getting angrier and angrier and your friend who is from India is not even aware of being late for you. "Man rules time. Time does not rule the Man" as opposed to "A stitch in time saves nine."

Time and Status

You judge how late you can be for an appointment based on your assessment of the status of the person you will meet. You can be late for your friends, but not for your boss.

High status people can be late for meetings with low status people, but not the other way around.

In monochronic cultures you telegraph to others how important you think they are to you

© ASDF_MEDIA /Shutterstock.com

by your promptness. Being late for an appointment is a sign of rudeness and lack of respect in mono-chronic cultures.

Time and Appropriateness

Cultural rules apply to the appropriate use of time. When meals are served, when you send out invitations for important events, when stores open and close, when alcohol is served, and when you eat particular foods, these are tied up in your culture's decisions about time and appropriateness.

Consider the following:

© Larissa-S/Shutterstock.com

Advance Notice

How long before an event you send out invitations signals the importance of the event. You can see this cue in play with the new "save the date" announcement. Such announcements tell you that a wedding invitation is forthcoming, so you had better "save the date" a year ahead of time so you can response "yes" to the invitation.

- In America wedding invitations are sent out six weeks before the wedding.
- Receiving an invitation at the three- or two-week mark signals that you are an after-thought even if you are not.

The amount of time you allow to elapse between receiving and answering a call or invitation sends a powerful nonverbal signal.

- Writing thank you notes.
- Answering an important phone call.
- Answering invitations.

These actions should be complete promptly. The promptness tells the receiver you care.

Appropriateness also addresses the question of when to contact others.

- When do you show up unannounced at someone's home?
- When are phone calls ok? Before 9 am? After 9 pm?
    - ❏ There are social conventions about this.
    - ❏ You need to find out what they are.

In the end, time tells you:

- what's important,
- your cultural background, and

- your geographic location (time and appropriateness is different in New York than in Salt Lake City).
  - ❏ People in New York come to parties late because it is expected.
  - ❏ In Salt Lake City, you come on time or a little early.

The big question about time is**:** Do you own your time? Your answer to this question will influence every other aspect of chronemics. So, do you own time?

GIFT-GIVING AS A NONVERBAL CUE

How does a gift work as a nonverbal cue? Well, gifts communicate.

- Feelings—we give gifts to people we like to let them know that.
- Nature of the relationship.

© Kostikova Natalia /Shutterstock.com

Expectations play a big role in gift-giving.

- We expect certain gifts based on relationships and appropriateness.
- We have expectations based on the event.
- We have expectations based on culture.

It is a true thing that you are not required to bring a gift to **any** event you attend and that includes weddings. A gift is not the price of admission, although many people think it is. You give a gift because you want to, not because you are forced to do so. But just try getting into a wedding without bring a gift.

Appropriateness is another consideration in gift-giving.

- How much is spent?
- The nature of the relationship.
  - ❏ Acquaintances give generic-type gifts that don't cost too much.
  - ❏ Intimates give more expensive and thought-out gifts.

It should not be surprising then that there are etiquette rules about gift-giving. The nature of the gift indicates the nature of the relationship. Certain gifts are considered inappropriate for single men to give single women, at least if you follow the old etiquette rules. Most of those prohibited gifts are clothing and jewelry.

Cultures have developed rules regarding gift-giving. Some of the comments above are based on the cultural expectations and appropriateness criteria of the United States. Clearly there is more to know.

Gift-Giving by Culture

Deploy your cell phone. Choose a culture and spend the next 10 minutes looking up the gift-giving style of that culture. Jot down a few examples. Then be prepared to discuss what you learned.

Business Gift-Giving.

Social Gift-Giving.

Chapter 8

"So listen, why don't you give me a call when you start taking things a little more seriously."

—The Joker, *The Dark Knight*

A Discussion of Listening

© Billion Photos/Shutterstock.com

EXCUSE ME WHILE I KISS THIS GUY

—Jimi Hendrix?

If you have ever thought that

- "hear the beat of the tangerine" was the actual lyric of *Dancing Queen* or that
- Taylor Swift sings "got a list of Starbuck lovers" in *Blank Spaces* or that
- Sir-Mix-A lot opined that "I like big butts in a can of limes" in *Baby Got Back*

then you are suffering from Kiss This Guy Syndrome. Urban Dictionary defines Kiss This Guy Syndrome as "A disorder believed to be the cause of misheard song lyrics.

There is a technical term for misheard lyrics. It's *mondegreens*. If you feel like it, wade through this article to learn more. http://www.newyorker.com/science/maria-konnikova/science-misheard-lyrics-mondegreens

Or go have some fun: http://www.kissthisguy.com/funny.php

The point of all this fun is that listening is not as easy as you might think. It actually takes some thought and more understanding. We listen all the time, but as you can see from Kiss This Guy, we often don't do it very well.

To become a better listener, you need to learn some things about yourself. Fill out the inventory below for a start.

INVENTORY

Thinking about yourself and how you communicate during the day, give the amount of time you spend each day doing the following communication activities.

Reading:

Writing:

Speaking:

Texting:

Viewing Social Media:

Listening:

Explain your numbers here:

If you gave the biggest percentage of your time to speaking you are not alone. Most people believe they talk far more than they do. You might respond that there is a study that shows that Americans spend on average 4.7 hours a day on their cell phones (digitaltrends n.d.). However, that 4.7 hours include checking social media and listening to others. You are not talking continually for those hours.

Listening is what you do most on a typical day. Listening is considered by some to be the most important communication skill you can master. Considering how much time you spend listening this should not come as a surprise. Here are some typical numbers (Emanuel et al. 2008).

- 11.4% Writing
- 16.1% Speaking
- 17.1% Reading
- 27.5% Interpersonal Listening
- 27.9% Media Listening

The numbers above are from one study, but you can go to almost any study of listening and get the same response. The numbers vary, but they overwhelmingly show that most of your communication time is spent listening.

Despite that fact that we spend so much time listening—some of us more than others, depending on the occupation you have—we receive virtually no training in listening. But this is a skill that requires lifelong practice. We begin by defining what we mean by listening.

DEFINITION

A transactional process in which a receiver attends and assigns meaning and responds to messages from others.

Let's break this down

- Listening is transactional because both sender and receiver are actively participating in the process.
- Listening requires that you acknowledge what the other is saying.
- Listening requires that an attempt at understanding is made.

© ESB Professional/Shutterstock.com

HEARING AND LISTENING

We often make the mistake of equating good listening with good hearing. We even talk about them as if they are equivalent. But in fact the two are very different.

Hearing is a biological process. Hearing is defined as the physical process of letting in audible stimuli without focusing on the stimuli. Sound comes to you and you hear. No understanding is necessary for hearing.

The definition of listening is entirely different. Listening requires understanding. And listening does not in fact require that you hear in the traditional sense many people use the word. The deaf community listens through signing.

© Tatiana Shepeleva/Shutterstock.com

THE PROCESS OF LISTENING

As you can probably guess listening is also a process. In some ways, it mirrors that communication process because both have the goal of meaning exchange. The process begins with:

© iQoncept/Shutterstock.com

Hear/Receive/Select

- Sorting through sounds.
- Observing nonverbal.
- Blocking out sounds you believe are irrelevant.

© RealVector/Shutterstock.com

Recall/Interpret/Understand

This is where you interpret what you attended to in the first step of the process.

You assign meaning to what you sense. At this point the process looks suspiciously like the Selective Attention step in the Perception Process.

For example: you are walking down the hall, not really focusing on any particular sound. It's all just a buzz to you. Suddenly you hear a group of sounds that sound suspiciously like your name. You are all of a sudden very attentive. Was that your name? Are these people talking about you?

You use who you are to interpret the message. Perception of the world around you and your perception of yourself are at work here.

Rate/Evaluate/Analyze

Now you begin evaluating the message. Questions arise:

- Is this message for me?
- Is this message positive or negative?
- Is this message important?
- What type of listening should I be doing here?

Response/Feedback

Your understanding of the message is your response. You have a lot of choices here about how you will respond.

Your response will depend on what choice you made about the type of listening you should be doing in this situation.

This is how listening works. But this does not tell you how well you listen or what your listening style is. And it does not tell you the level at which you listen to any given message.

WHY WE LISTEN

Part of your responsibility as a communicator is to ask "why" questions. In the case of listening the "why" question is simple: "Why am I listening in this particular situation?" Your answer to this question will influence

- Your level of involvement in the communication situation.
- The type of listening you will do in this situation.
- What you will listen for in this situation.

Here are some of the reasons we listen:

For Enjoyment

When you listen to simply enjoy the world around you, you don't ask much of the communication situation. All you want is to engage some emotion or relax or maybe just be entertained.

You are not overly involved in this listening situation. You may even tune out for a while and not even realize it.

For Appreciation

Your purpose here is not just to enjoy on a surface level. You gather information so you better understand what you are listening to. Such listening brings a deeper kind of enjoyment. You listen to music or watch and listen to TV and films this way? You listen for

- The beauty of the music. The emotions the music draws from you.
- You listen for the structure of music or of language.

Because you are listening for specific things when you listen to enjoy, you need to be listening more carefully. Your level of involvement is higher here than in listening for enjoyment. You may even decide that you need to be on the level of analysis if you really wish to appreciate a song or story.

For Comprehension

One reason you listen is so you can understand. You need information to do your job better or help someone out or to acquire knowledge. This is listening for comprehension. You do this in class. You listen to those things you do not yet understand so you can master them.

You have to be fairly well engaged in the listening situation in order to listen to understand. Concentration, picking out key words and ideas so you know what is important requires a fair amount of attention.

You know what happens when you let your mind wander in class.

© igorstevanovic/Shutterstock.com

For Analysis

You listen to a speech and want to decide whether or not to believe it.

You listen to a salesperson and decide if you will buy the product.

You may listen to evaluate in order to decide if you are the best person to answer someone's question.

You must evaluate what you hear to make a good decision. This requires a high level of listening involvement. You need to listen to understand the message. Once understanding is reached you then need to go one step further and draw conclusions from what you have heard.

© theromb/Shutterstock.com

For Identification

You use sounds to figure out what is going on.

You know how your car engine sounds and you become used to that sound. When the sounds change you something is up.

You hear odd noises at night. This makes you nervous because you know how your house is supposed to sound and it doesn't sound like this!

You listen to the vocal inflection of others to gauge how they are feeling or what they are thinking. When vocal inflection is all you have by way of nonverbal cues—you are on the phone with someone—listening for identification is especially important.

© yevgeniy11/Shutterstock.com

All of the above examples require analysis. You have to think through what you are hearing and figure out what it means. The level of listening involvement is high.

For Empathy

You listen as a counselor or friend.

This is what friends do when one is having a problem and the other is there as a sounding board.

You might have a sibling that you confide in.

The purpose of listening for empathy is to feel as others feel so you can understand them better.

If you decide you want to listen for empathy you need to be totally engaged with the listening situation. You will find out why in minutes.

© Ljupco Smokovski/Shutterstock.com

For Self-Understanding

You listen to others to help you grow personally. While you should not listen to everything every freelance critic has to say about you, you should pick out a few trustworthy people and listen to what they have to say.

You should also listen closely to how you sound to the world around you. You project an image to the world by what comes out of your mouth. People then assess you based on what you say and how you sound when you say it.

Listen to yourself. Then ask yourself:

© Bruce Rolff/Shutterstock.com

- How do I sound to myself?
  - ❏ Cynical
  - ❏ Sarcastic
  - ❏ Happy
  - ❏ Interested in life
- How do I sound to others?
  - ❏ Interested in them
  - ❏ Depressed
  - ❏ Bored
  - ❏ Friendly
- Can others gauge, by how I talk, what I think or feel about
  - ❏ People
  - ❏ Issues
  - ❏ My job

- Do I like the way I sound?
    - ❏ Does how I talk truly represent who I am?
    - ❏ Am I expressing myself in a way that hides who I am?
    - ❏ Is my way of talking helping or hurting my interpersonal relationship?

The better you understand this, the more likely you are to communicate well with others. If you are listening to understand yourself, you are going to need to be fully engaged in the listening situation.

HOW WE LISTEN

Listening provides you with yet another set of choices. How exactly will you listen in a particular communication situation? Does this situation call for you to marshal the skills of

- Content listening,
- Critical listening, or
- Empathic listening?

Each of these types has different rules and skills that apply to them. Using empathic skills in a critical listening situation is not going to get you very far. You would not, for example, pull out a notebook and pen when your significant other comes home and sits down to talk about the day. You would pull out that notebook if you were in class.

CONTENT LISTENING

Content listening is listening for information.

- You need to write down notes for a class.
- You need to ask your supervisor for the answer to a question.
- You ask for directions to a specific place.
- Your boss gives you a task.

In all of these situations you are engaged in content listening. The purpose of this type of listening is to gather information. You will use this information in different ways, but the point remains the same. When listening for information you are not analyzing the content of what you hear. That is a different type of listening.

The skills you will need to do this type of listening well are:

- Note-taking. You may have learned in a Study Skills class how to do this or you may have designed your own notes. Good note-taking includes:
  - ❏ Understanding what the central idea is.
  - ❏ Identifying the main points.
  - ❏ Identifying the sub-points.
  - ❏ Identifying what is important to the speaker.
- Questioning for clarification and definition.
- Paraphrasing to indicate that you understood the message.

CRITICAL LISTENING

Critical listening is listening to analyze. This type of listening requires you to go a step beyond listening for content. You gather information and then you decide whether this information is good or bad, true or not, helpful or not. You analyze what you hear. You are not likely to use this type of listening unless you are concerned about the accuracy of information.

© Denis Simonov/Shutterstock.com

You engage in critical listening when

- You are listening to the person trying to sell you a car.
- You are listening to the person trying to get your vote.
- Your friend is trying to convince you to go see *John Wick 2*.
- It's two in the morning and you and your friends are arguing about who is better, LeBron James or Kobe Bryant.

Critical listening begins with content listening and then adds the following:

- Question what you hear. Don't take things at face value.
- Evaluate material and reach your own conclusions about it.
- Be receptive to new ideas and information.
- Demand that assertions and opinions be supported by facts.
- Evaluate the credibility of the sources speakers use.
- Be skeptical of vague or incomprehensible language.

These skills may sound harsh and cruel in interpersonal relationships, but critical listening is not a negative skill. It will help you determine more accurately what the speaker wants and how to deal with the speaker on this subject and with this message.

REFLECTIVE OR EMPATHIC LISTENING

In reflective or empathic listening you are listening for feelings and responding to them. Remember the discussion about messages having both a content and emotional level? Empathic listening situations concentrate on the emotional level of messages.

You engage in empathic listening when:

- You are listening to a friend's troubles.
- You are listening to your elderly parent's worries about health.
- You are listening to your child's school day woes.

We are not talking sympathy here. Sympathy is a feeling of pity or compassion. Empathy means you actively try to feel what the other person is feeling.

In the context of empathic or reflective listening, empathy is a process that includes

- Figuring out that someone is in an emotional state.
- Identifying what that state is.
- Responding to that state appropriately.

Empathic or reflective listening has two main elements:

- Recognizing another person's feelings and
- Responding appropriately to those feelings.

Since all aspects of communication are intertwined it should be pointed out here that the people best suited to do empathic or reflective listening are high self-monitored people. Such people are able to assess verbal and nonverbal cues well and respond appropriately to them.

Beyond message and self-concept, empathic or reflective listening also involves perception. The perception process leaps into action as we assess and selectively attend to

- gestures,
- facial expressions,
- language use,
- vocal inflection, and so on.

We then organize this information to interpret the person's emotional state.

While empathic or reflective listening is transactional or needs to be in order for meaning to be exchanged, the actors in this drama are not equal. Empathic or reflective listening is *you* **oriented**. The Empathic Listener is not concerned with him or herself, but with the speaker.

EMPATHIC LISTENING AND HOW TO DO IT

You might want to use the following outline to help you develop into a good empathic listener.

© arloo/Shutterstock.com

Decide if you should get involved

Not everyone is good at empathic listening. Learn enough about yourself to decide if you are a person who can do this.

If you are good at empathy you need to ask if you are the appropriate person to listen in a given communication situation. You may not want to listen to the problem your friend is having with a significant other because you are also friends with that person. TMI! Once you decide you can be helpful, the next step is:

© Paranamir/Shutterstock.com

Sort out the problem

People usually engage in empathic or reflective listening when a problem crops up that needs a solution. Your job as the listener is to probe for information. That information should lead the speaker to the problem.

© dizain/Shutterstock.com

Choose a course of action

Once the problem has been outlined a satisfying resolution is possible. Now is the time to help the speaker discover how many and what kind of solutions to the problem are possible.

It is not your job to choose that solution for the speaker. Your job is to help the speaker make a choice. The speaker doesn't own the choice if the speaker doesn't make it.

Cheerlead

Summarize and help the speaker feel good about the conclusion of the problem.

Encourage follow up so the speaker can talk about the successful conclusion to the problem or that you are available to go through all this again if the solution doesn't work.

EMPATHIC LISTENING SKILLS

Empathic listening is not easy. It takes time and effort. But it may be the only way available to you to help the speaker.

Empathic listening skills are in a class of their own. You may apply the content listening skill of gathering information and the critical listening skill of analyzing what you hear so you can better respond, the skills used for empathic listening are materially different than other skills. They are

THE DO-BEHAVIORS

Do care

If you really don't care, then don't engage in empathic listening.

If you can't manage to understand or feel the feelings of another then don't engage in empathic listening.

© Chinnapong/Shutterstock.com

Do respond in a thoughtful manner

Don't monopolize the conversation.

Be specific in what you say.

Try to accurately recall the message sent.

Monitor your nonverbal cues so they make sense in the context.

© Monkey Business Images/Shutterstock.com

Do use subtle ways to encourage the speaker to continue

Use verbal and nonverbal cues.

Verbal: "go on"; "Tell me more"; "That's interesting."

Nonverbal: a nod; direct eye contact, touching.

© ESB Professional /Shutterstock.com

Do use your voice to convey empathy

Use your voice to convey your feelings to the speaker. Let the speaker know you catch the feelings of the listener.

Refer to the information in the chapter on vocalics to help you develop an empathic vocal style.

© Ollyy/Shutterstock.com

Do vary your responses

You telegraph lack of interest and/or understanding when you use the same verbal and nonverbal cues as your response to the speaker.

Vocal variety, word choice, nodding, or other ways of indicating you are listening should reflect what is happening in the empathic listening situation.

© dizain/Shutterstock.com

THE DON'T-BEHAVIORS

Don't tell the speaker you know how the speaker feels

The importance of this "don't" cannot be overstated. Everyone experiences life differently. You may have had an experience similar to the one the speaker is discussing, but they are not the same. You will not feel the same emotions in the same way. That's for starters.

Second, the speaker may not want to hear about your problem. The speaker wants center stage. By agreeing to engage in empathic listening you have agreed that the speaker is the center of attention. Minimize you.

© pathdoc/Shutterstock.com

Don't dismiss feelings with trite retorts

"Life's like that";

"Life's just one damn thing after another";

"You'll get over it";

"There are a lot of fish in the ocean."

This doesn't help much does it? Such remarks dismiss the feelings and make them inconsequential.

© file404/Shutterstock.com

Don't minimize how the speaker feels

It really doesn't help to tell a speaker "Don't feel that way" or "It isn't all that important" or "I don't know what all the fuss is about."

People can't help how they feel. They can help how they respond to feelings, but they are going to feel. Telling them not to is not very helpful.

© Jakub Krechowicz/Shutterstock.com

Don't evaluate or critique

You are not engaged in critical listening here. Do not pass judgment. You don't have to like what the speaker is telling you but you have to understand it.

© Borysevych.com/Shutterstock.com

Don't give advice

The speaker may not want advice. The speaker may not be able to take the advice. You don't know the whole story so your advice may be dangerous or unhelpful.

If the speaker takes your advice and it doesn't work the speaker will not have ownership of the result and blame you. If the speaker takes your advice and it does work the speaker will not feel good about it because the speaker will not have ownership of the result. Either way, advice is a dangerous thing.

"Elves seldom give unguarded advice, for advice is a dangerous gift, even from the wise to the wise, and all courses may run ill."—Gildor Inglorion (Tolkien 2000)

Don't pretend to listen

Look at this guy on the phone. Do you think he is paying attention to the person making the call? He seems much more interested in what is going on on that tablet.

You can also have the problem of losing the thread of what another is saying. You daydream. If this happens ask the speaker to repeat the message. Faking understanding if caught will poison the situation.

BENEFITS OF LISTENING EFFECTIVELY

What's in it for you? Why should you study listening? Below are some answers to those questions.

Effective listening helps you learn

First, you will benefit from the insights and experiences of others. Obviously, if you are listening with intent to others you will learn things you did not know before.

Good listening helps you in the classroom. It is certainly easier to pass a class if you are using good listening skills well.

© LStockStudio/Shutterstock.com

Effective listening helps you solve problems

You will have listened well and been able to see problems coming. You have to listen well to even know that there is a problem. Listening to yourself and others will help you generate solutions.

Do you think the guy on the left thought out the chair problem on his own? Maybe. But it is more likely he had listened at one time to somebody talk about how to think out of the box.

© gualtiero boffi/Shutterstock.com

Effective listening helps you make good decisions

You will get more information, be able to sort out the information you receive and therefore make better decisions.

In the TV series *Leverage* Elliott always beats Hardison at *Rock, Paper, Scissors* because Hardison has a tell. Listening effectively, which includes assessing nonverbal, is helpful in all sorts of situations.

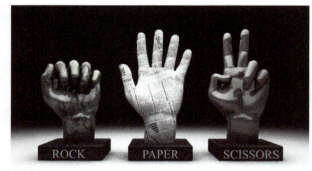

© Inked Pixels/Shutterstock.com

Effective listening helps you become a good leader

The connecting concept in this photograph is listening. A good leader is a good listener.

Even if the leader never takes up a suggestion of the group, if the group thinks it is being listened to, the group will be satisfied.

People want to be heard. A good leader understands that and works to make it happen.

Effective listening helps you become a desirable companion

The most charming person at a party is likely the one who is doing none of the talking. It is the person doing the listening, asking questions, responding with interest to what is said.

One of the ways you show you care is by listening to others, putting them at the center of attention.

BARRIERS TO EFFECTIVE LISTENING

Practice makes permanent as the saying goes. And you have been practicing your poor listening skills for a very long time. Now it is time to throw off those habits and learn how to listen more effectively. Below are behaviors in which you engage all the time. You are doing it now. We need to confront our poor listening habits, define them, and find ways to overcome them. Poor listening habits are:

Ambushing

You listen only so you can attack the speaker. You actually listen carefully but only to gather information with which to attack the speaker.

© Sergey Zaykov/Shutterstock.com

Arguing with the Speaker's Logic

When you hear something you don't like you begin to make arguments in your head to refute what you are hearing. If you don't listen to the complete message you may end up responding to a message that was not sent.

Keep an open mind. You may disagree with what you are hearing, but let the speaker finish before you start objecting.

© arek_malang/Shutterstock.com

Confirmation Bias

Check out the websites you visit and where you get your news. Does it seem that these sources all have the same point of view? They probably do because in general we practice confirmation bias.

You tend to listen to messages that support what you already think. That's confirmation bias.

© Kheng Guan Toh/Shutterstock.com

Defensive Listening

You perceive a hostile, attacking message when none was intended. When you are in a heightened emotional state you may view anything that is said as an attack. Even a pleasant "Good Morning" can be viewed as hostile if you want to view it that way.

© Dragon Images/Shutterstock.com

Denying the Difference

People bring their beliefs, attitudes, values, behaviors, and experiences to the table in every communication situation. Those BAVBEs have an effect on how people listen.

Also, different situations call for different listening styles and skills.

Your job as a listener is to figure out what listening you are supposed to be doing—content, critical, or empathic—and how the BAVBEs of the people in the situation affect their listening and use that information to improve your listening ability.

© oneinchpunch/Shutterstock.com

Filling in the Gaps

When you finish the speaker's sentences you are filling in the gaps rather than letting the speaker finish the message.

Adding information that the speaker hasn't given you is another instance of this barrier.

MIND THE GAP

© pisaphotography/Shutterstock.com

Insensitive Listening

When you engage in insensitive listening you do not pay attention to verbal and nonverbal cues that could affect the message. Insensitive listeners often ignore nonverbal cues. They respond to the content level of the message when the emotional level is the one that needs the response.

© Daren Woodward/Shutterstock.com

Laziness

If you believe that listening involves no work, then you are probably a lazy listener.

You let the message flow over you but make no effort to understand what is said.

I may look lazy, but I'm just contemplating.

© Sari ONeal/Shutterstock.com

Message Overload

You have had this happen to you in class. Your professor is droning on and getting faster and faster in delivery. There is too much coming at you too fast. You shut down.

© edeantoine/Shutterstock.com

Preoccupation

You are so concentrated on your own problems or interests that you block out what others are saying.

It's not that you don't care, it's just that your mind keeps wandering back to your own troubles or concerns. For example, it is very difficult to listen effectively to someone when you are in a hurry.

© Valery Sidelnykov/Shutterstock.com

Pseudolistening

This is one of the habits you have practiced the longest and are probably most adept at. You engage in this behavior because you are not really interested in what is being said but you have to appear to be.

You make the appropriate responses, but are disengaged from the listening experience. Nodding your head. Saying, "Uh Huh."

Look at this guy in the photo. This guy. He is probably thinking about lunch.

© Air Images/Shutterstock.com

Rapid Thought

Our brains can process about 450–500 words per minute. Generally, people speak at 120–150 wpm. We have a lot of spare brain time. And because of that we have a tendency to fade out when people talk.

© Trimitrius/Shutterstock.com

Also, our brains can function on many levels of attentiveness at the same time. If you came from a large, talkative family you probably have the ability to listen and respond to several conversations at once. This listening habit is very difficult to control.

Responding Emotionally

Remember when we talked about noise in the channel way back in Chapter 2? We discussed red flag and green flag words. We discussed that again in the chapter on verbal communication. Now is your chance to put that barrier into practice.

When responding emotionally you let your feelings get in the way of meaning exchange.

© WAYHOME studio/Shutterstock.com

Stage Hogging

Look at this young woman. It looks like she hasn't gotten a word in edgewise for hours. This man is talking, talking, talking. If she did get the chance to speak it looks like this guy will use that to jump off to something else to talk about.

Stage hogs like to hear themselves talk. You are a prop.

© Rommel Canlas/Shutterstock.com

Selective Listening

You listen to those parts of the message that you like and block out the rest.

Children do this all the time. Children don't hear "Clean up your room." They hear "And then you can have a cookie."

We listen to TV programs, but not commercials. Or the other way round.

© visualgang /Shutterstock.com

Thinking before You Listen

You are so anxious to get in what you want to say that you begin formulating your answer before the speaker has finished the message.

Were you the person in class with the hand raised before the teacher even asked the questions? The Hermione Granger of the class?

© Alex Brylov/Shutterstock.com

BEGIN DEMOLISHING LISTENING BARRIERS

Make listening work for you. Understand your poor listening habits. Look at the good habits and work on those. Here are some tips to help you become a better listener.

© Gwoeii/Shutterstock.com

Adapt

There is no one best listening strategy. Not all will be appropriate for each listening situation. Your responsibility is to decide which strategy is best for you in any given situation and use it.

Be aware of the differences in people, context, and goals. Notice how different situations call for different listening skills and apply those.

© Photosebia/Shutterstock.com

Control Obstacles

We talked about this earlier when we discussed noise in the channel. Your first job in any communication situation is to analyze the barriers—the noise—and minimize it. Look for those things that will be a distraction and work to eliminate them.

© Dean Drobot/Shutterstock.com

Corral Your Brain

While there is not a lot you can do to control rapid thought, there is one thing you could try. Make it a practice to monitor your thoughts as you listen. Be aware of when you start to fade out. The sooner you fade back in the more success you will have in communication.

© Ivan Popovych/Shutterstock.com

Engage

You have practiced your poor listening habits for a long time. You have to disengage your poor listening habits and engage the good ones. Listen carefully, even if the material is difficult. Don't give up on it. Stay focused.

© Gustavo Frazao/Shutterstock.com

Find the Benefit

Listening well is hard work. Finding some benefit in the message helps keep you up to the hard work of listening.

You may have to struggle to find a benefit in listening in some situations. In class, for example, you may wonder what good this information is going to do you. Well, perhaps it will allow you to pass the next exam.

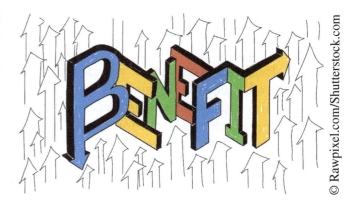

© Rawpixel.com/Shutterstock.com

Participate

The communication process is two-way. As a listener you have as much responsibility to the communication situation as the speaker has.

If you are not listening, you are not going to be able to give feedback, define the barriers to good communication, or accurately receive the message.

Use all communication/listening skills available in that situation.

© Syda Productions/Shutterstock.com

Physically Pay Attention

It helps if your body plays along with your listening. Look at the people in this photograph. The young woman and the man next to her are looking up at the speaker. The bearded man is leaning forward. The man in the lower left corner has a paper and pen ready for note-taking.

An alert posture helps you concentrate. You are more likely to daydream when you are in a relaxed posture.

As with most things, in communication there is no one "right way" to physically pay attention. The context certainly plays a role as does your personal belief about what "physically paying attention" means.

© Rawpixel.com/Shutterstock.com

- You can close your eyes if it helps you listen more attentively.
- You can lean back if that helps.
- You can doodle.

Be aware however that those around you may interpret these behaviors as being nonengaged.

Repetition

This skill helps you focus your attention as you repeat what you have heard. If you can do this it lets people know you are paying attention. Repetition helps when you have to write down specific information—you repeat the information aloud for reassurance that you are correct. Repetition helps you remember someone's name.

Paraphrasing

Paraphrasing is a type of feedback that restates the message in your own words. You engage in paraphrasing if you are not quite sure you understand the message and are looking for confirmation. Paraphrasing is a better response than "WHAT?"

Paraphrasing gives the speaker response options.

The photo is a paraphrase of the famous fresco on the ceiling of the Sistine Chapel in Rome that depicts God creating Adam. Here is the original: https://en.wikipedia.org/wiki/Gallery_of_Sistine_Chapel_ceiling#/media/File:Adam_na_restauratie.jpg

There are ways to go about paraphrasing. You have to choose the one that best fits the communication situation in which you find yourself and which part of the message you wish to respond to. You can paraphrase for

- Content
- Feeling

In the photograph above the artist is paraphrasing Michelangelo's understanding of how God created humanity. The artist believes, apparently, that Michelangelo identifies with God's creative. The artist suggests that God's creative act is like a painter's creative act. This is an example of paraphrasing for feeling.

Questioning

Any good lawyer will tell you that you never ask a question you don't already know the answer to. That is sound advice in a courtroom, but not so much in life in general.

© Rawpixel.com/Shutterstock.com

You have to know what information you want before you can ask a good question. Then you have to frame that question in a way that gets you the answer you are looking for.

That "what?" you respond with almost automatically is not a well-framed question.

We ask questions for three reasons:

■ To gather information
■ To clarify
■ To define

Making the correct choice of question can be the difference between exchange meaning or remaining clueless.

Suspend Judgment

This is a skill most associated with empathic listening. Wait to hear out the speaker. Avoid analyzing the speaker's feelings. Keep an open mind until you have all the information you need to form an opinion.

© Alex Staroseltsev/Shutterstock.com

Note-Taking

Do not be afraid to take notes. It is helpful for memory and retention. Some people find it difficult to concentrate on note-taking and listening at the same time. But it is a useful skill if you can master it. It also helps you to focus attention as the notes can act as a substitute for the speaker.

© George Rudy/Shutterstock.com

Use Information Recall Aids

Whatever it takes to recall information use it.

- Rhymes
- Mnemonic devises
- Association

People who are good at recalling names aren't superheroes. They just have a good store of recall devices they tap when they need them.

© Ahmet Misirligul/Shutterstock.com

Chapter 9

"I'm gonna make him an offer he can't refuse."

—Don Vito Corleone, *The Godfather*

A Discussion of Conflict Management

© ArchMan/Shutterstock.com

Interpersonal conflict exists when people who depend on each other have differing views, interests, or goals.

What we know about conflict is this:

- It is a normal, inevitable part of all interpersonal relationships.
- Conflict does not necessarily indicate that a relationship is unhealthy or in trouble.
- It is both overt and covert.
  - Overt. It is out in the open both verbally and nonverbally.
  - Covert. Sometimes this means the conflict is also unacknowledged. Passive or aggressive behavior is usually disguised or denied conflict.
- Can be managed well or managed poorly.
  - Managed well conflict can result in deepening the bonds of a relationship.
  - Managed poorly conflict can result in splitting a relationship apart.

Let's look at a definition of interpersonal conflict. This definition comes to us from William Wilmot and Joyce Hocker (2013) and it states:

Conflict is expressed struggle between at least two interdependent parties who perceive incompatible goals, scarce resources/rewards, and interference from the other party in achieving their goals.

Breaking it down, we see:

© Solcan Sergiu/Shutterstock.com

Expressed Struggle

The parties to the conflict are generally emotionally and personally invested in the struggle. The stakes are high.

We are not talking here about casual disagreements—what do you want for dinner tonight; mild differences—you say tomato, I say tomahto; or intellectual arguments—people are born good. No, people are born evil.

An expressed struggle can be
- verbal
  - loaded words
  - hurtful words.
- nonverbal
  - sarcasm
  - facial expressions
  - the silent treatment
  - out-of-control screaming match.

© WAYHOME studio/Shutterstock.com

Interdependence

You have noticed that when you are in a relationship you and the other person in the relationship rely on each other.

This reliance takes the form of emotional support, financial support, spiritual support, you know, all those needs we talked about earlier.

The degree to which you are dependent on the other party in achieving your goals is a factor in interpersonal conflict.

© Lightspring/Shutterstock.com

Perceived Incompatible Goals, Scarce Resources or Rewards

The emphasis here is on the word, "perceived." In the Perception chapter, we talked about how people see the world differently. The conflicts you have are essentially a perception issue.

- **Goals:** You want to start your own recording company with the goal of becoming a music big shot. Your significant other's goal is a stable income stream. Conflict ensues.
- **Scarce Resources:** You want to buy a fabulous car. Your significant other wants to pay the rent. There is not enough money to do both. Scarce resources also include time, affection, and space.

© Sue Newcomb/Shutterstock.com

Look at this example:

Colton loves country music and Colton's friend Tyrone is a huge hip-hop fan. They are not roommates and don't attend concerts together and make it a point to not talk much about music. It is safe to assume their differences about music will not cause much conflict. If neither one has the goal of changing the other's mind about music or if neither one has the goal of getting the other to a concert, there will be no conflict.

Perceived Interference of Goal Achievement

It's one thing to feel that your goals are not compatible with the goals of your significant or the goals of a friend. After all, you can work those things out, like Colton and Tyrone did by simply avoiding the area of conflict.

© Sergey Nivens/Shutterstock.com

But if you add to the incompatibility, the perception that the other party is somehow **preventing** you from achieving your goals, that becomes one more step toward conflict.

Imagine your college roommates don't seem to care about making the Dean's List this semester as much as you do. You feel your roommates' penchant for throwing all night beer parties in the suite prevents you from studying and getting to bed at a decent hour. You have got a conflict.

Now that you have a definition of interpersonal conflict, try working with it. Read the story below and then briefly describe how Bryant's situation with his parents qualifies as an interpersonal conflict according to the definition.

Bryant wants to attend Howard University in Washington DC. However, his parents are against him attending a college so far away from their home in Honolulu. He feels that he should be allowed to attend any school he desires since he has been awarded a Bill and Melinda Gates Foundation full scholarship. However, Bryant is the oldest of six children and his parents can't imagine their 17-year-old son living so far from home. They argue that they can't afford to fly him home on holidays and summer vacations and if there were an emergency, they would be too far away to help.

Bryant angrily calls them paranoid "helicopter" parents who won't allow him to follow his dreams. He has stomped around the house for weeks giving his parents the silent treatment, and feels they are being totally unreasonable. His parents are visibly frustrated and upset by his insistence on considering only one university even though his scholarship will allow him to attend any university, including the University of Hawaii where he can continue to live at home and work in the family restaurant. Having never left the island, his parents have always heard about the 'chaos and crime' of big cities like Washington DC.

Time is running out and the Gates Foundation needs the family to decide

Describe expressed struggle:

_____

_____

_____

_____

_____

Describe incompatible goals and interference:

_____
_____
_____
_____
_____

Describe interdependence:

_____
_____
_____
_____
_____

AREAS OF CONFLICT

We have already established that interpersonal conflict is about perception. That means that you can get into conflict over just about anything. You know people who do that. You know people who are always ready for a fight. Then there are those who avoid conflict. It is not that they won't engage if they think it is worthwhile, it's that they hold back for the really important issues.

© Suat Gursozlu/Shutterstock.com

Read that last sentence again. Perception plays a role in what you think is important and what you are willing to go to the wall for and what you aren't.

Your Conflict Continuum

Fill in the blanks:

I never get into conflict over:

I sometimes get into conflict over:

I always get into conflict over:

Knowing what lights you up and what doesn't will help you manage your conflicts more effectively. We can look at this another way. Here is a continuum that show you why you will get into conflict about some things and not others.

Another Way to Look at The Conflict Continuum		
Minor differences	to	Highly Emotional
Non-competitive	to	Highly Competitive
Non-violent	to	Violent

You might think something is a minor difference while your friend thinks the end of the world is nigh. You don't want to compete, your friend does. You are passive, your friend is not about an issue. Conflict ensues.

So, what does cause all that trouble in our relationships? Here we go:

Relationship Definition

Conflicts arise when parties to the relationship have different ideas about exactly what that relationship is.

Studies show that men and women living together in a romantic relationship have a very different understanding of what "living together" means. For women, it means getting married. For men, it means living together (Diane Swanbrow, 2011).

Another example would be your understanding of your friendship and your friend's understanding. You may think you are casual friends and so don't call or text every day. Your friend may think you are intimate friends and want that every day call. Conflict ensues.

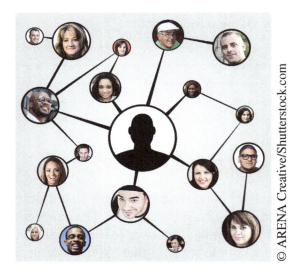

© ARENA Creative/Shutterstock.com

Individual Differences

Your personality, how you think about things and how you respond to others is a source of conflict.

Your habits are also a source of friction in relationships. Being late all the time, not dropping the toilet seat, not cleaning up after yourself are all area of conflict.

© Ruslan Grumble/Shutterstock.com

Personal Criticism

Constant critical assessment of friends and loved ones can be a source of conflict. You don't like to be criticized. You especially don't like to be criticized for something over which you have no control.

Being criticized for your weight is not helpful if you have been trying and failing to lose the extra pounds.

Your expectations about chores and how they should be done can lead to rousing conflicts

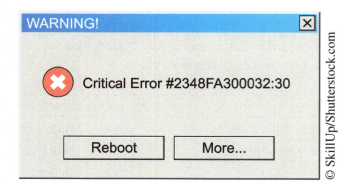

© SkillUp/Shutterstock.com

over how precisely to fill the dishwasher. The most fun is vacuuming again after your roommate or significant other just finished the job because "it wasn't done right."

Money

People fight about money for a variety of reasons. Those reasons revolve around how each person in the relationship perceives money.

- Are you frugal or a spendthrift?
- Should you spend or save or do both?
- What is money for?

Your answers to these questions will explain to you why you and your friends or significant other fight about money.

© givaga/Shutterstock.com

Sex

- Who with?
- When?
- How much?

Individuals understand sex in different ways. When those ways collide, you get conflict.

© AS Inc/Shutterstock.com

Who Does What

You grew up in a house where chores were done in certain ways by certain people. You bring those expectations to your new relationships.

Think about your family.

- Whose job was it to take out the garbage?
- Whose job was it to vacuum and dust?
- Whose job was it to clean up after dinner?

You bring the expectation that these things will be done the same way by the same people into your relationships—friends, roommates, and significant other. When those expectations are not met, there is conflict.

© Angela Waye/Shutterstock.com

Decision-making

How decisions are made in your relationships is also a source of conflict. The conflict can arise from:

© travellight/Shutterstock.com

- One person insisting on making all decisions.
- Both people insisting that they both make decisions.
- One person refusing to make decisions.
- Both people refusing to make decisions.

FACTORS THAT INFLUENCE CONFLICT

Interpersonal conflicts are not all the same. Remember the continuum above? They can take the form of

© ibreakstock/Shutterstock.com

- Minor differences: What to have for dinner?
- Competition: Who gets the highest grade?
- Emotional unhappiness: You want more affection from your partner.
- Nonviolent discussion: I want to go to Aruba. Let's talk.
- Violent: Domestic abuse.

Following are some variables that influence the way people manage conflict.

Communication Climate

As you will see, when you get to the Relationship chapter, the communication climate is the social tone that permeates a relationship.

The communication that people share sets that tone. If shared verbal and nonverbal messages are perceived to be positive, we feel valued and supported and may describe the overall relationship as warm and sunny and may be inclined to respond to conflict in more positive ways.

© Igor Zh./Shutterstock.com

On the other hand, those in an abusive relationship may feel disrespected and ignored, and may describe the climate in the relationship as cold, dark, and stormy! Conflict interaction in those relationships may be noticeably more negative by comparison.

Gender

How men and women handle conflict has been studied over many decades. There is some disagreement to the extent of how gender influences conflict. We know that they do, however, social scientists suggest gender differences are relatively small.

Here is a little chart that shows some of the difference between men's and women's conflict styles.

© chrupka/Shutterstock.com

Men	Women
More Competitive.	Inclined to cooperate to maintain the relationship.
Tends to take a more aggressive stance.	Inclined to take an indirect aggressive stance.
Demanding (not inclined to offer an explanation).	Inclined to accommodate rather than compete directly.

Culture

One of your cultures is that of your family. Families have individual ways of engaging in conflict.

If you come from a high-conflict home, you are likely to see conflict as a normal way to communicate. If you come from a low-conflict home, you may wish to avoid conflict at all costs.

Cultures in which honor is a prized attribute have different ways of dealing with conflict. Duels, blood feuds, and social stigma are all conflict strategies in honor-valuing cultures.

The Individualistic or Collectivist culture continuum will influence you as well. As members of an individualistic culture, Americans understand that they have rights. Conflict is a good strategy to protect those rights (Ting-Toomey, 1985). Since the group takes precedence in the collectivist culture, conflict can be seen as disrupting group harmony and putting oneself above the group (Gudykunstand Kim, 2003).

© Rawpixel.com/Shutterstock.com

Technology or Social Media

Media and technology has had a tremendous effect on our ability to interact and communicate. In a conflict situation, the choices you make are important.

Do you meet face-to-face or do you email or call on the phone? Each of those choices reflect your feelings regarding the conflict.

Have you ever left a voicemail rather than speak to your friend? Perhaps you wanted to avoid a possible conflict you felt was going to happen if you actually talked to your friend, so you hid behind the technology. It is much easier to say "no" over voicemail!

© Rawpixel.com/Shutterstock.com

- Don't press send unless you are sure you really want to say what is in that email.
- Don't expect emojis to truly convey your emotions.
- Don't think 140 characters in a twitter message is adequate for important communication

CONFLICT STYLES

In a conflict situation, the choices you make are important. The choices you make in response will influence what happens next.

- Will there be an escalation of tensions?
- Will there be movement toward collaboration?

We generally manage conflict by resorting to one of five primary conflict styles:

© ibreakstock/Shutterstock.com

- avoiding,
- accommodating,
- competing,
- compromising,
- collaborating.

These five styles are influenced by culture and social expectations as well as context and situation. Each has its own advantages and disadvantages.

Each conflict management style exists at the intersection of the degree of one's concern for self (personal goals) and the degree of one's concern for the other's goals (McCorkle and Reese, 2010).

Avoidance

Low concern for our own goals as well as low concern for the goals of the other party will often lead to *avoidance* (or withdrawal) of conflict.

This is considered a lose–lose situation because neither party will have realized their goals.

Avoidance is not always a bad strategy. When might avoidance be a good idea?

© pathdoc/Shutterstock.com

Accommodation

If you have low concern for your own goals, and high concern for the goals of the other, the result will be an *accommodation* to the other's wishes.

This is a lose–win situation because the other's goals are realized at the expense of your own.

You might adopt this strategy when you are minimally attached to a goal at a particular time. Or, the goal you want is not as important to you as your friend's or significant other's is.

© ESB Professional/Shutterstock.com

Competition

High concern for yourself and low concern for the goals of the other will result in *competition.* This is a win–lose situation because your "win" is dependent on the other losing.

Many people look at conflict like this. One person must win and the other has to lose. This style is not helpful as one of the conflictees is going to go away unhappy. In such cases, the conflict is not over. It will most likely pop up again as one person believes the conflict has not been resolved.

© Vaselyev Alexandr/Shutterstock.com

Compromise

Moderate concern for self, as well as the other tends toward *compromise* with the result that each one gives a little to gain a little.

However, this is considered a "negotiated" lose–lose because no one's goals are fully realized.

© zimmytws/Shutterstock.com

Collaboration

When you have a high concern for your self-interest and you couple that with a high concern for the goals of the other party, the result will be a move toward *collaboration* where the needs of both parties are met.

This is considered a win–win as both people in the conflict believe their goals have been met.

© Rawpixel.com/Shutterstock.com

COMPLEMENTARY AND SYMMETRICAL CONFLICT

In our relationships, the approaches to conflict we use can either be complementary or symmetrical.

- Complementary:
  - ❑ Positive Complementary Approach uses different but mutually reinforcing behaviors.
  - ❑ Destructive Complementary Approach uses different but mutually negative reinforcing behaviors.

© Antonio Guillem/Shutterstock.com

- Symmetrical:
  - ❑ Both choose the same tactics.
  - ❑ For instance, your roommate makes fun of your music choices in front of group your roommate's friends. You in turn joke in front of your friends about your roommate's inability to master the basics of the guitar even after five years of lessons. This is considered destructive symmetry.

Notice the example of complementary and symmetrical conflict with Mazie and Daisy who we see above at their desk:

Potential Conflict Situation	Complementary Conflict	Symmetrical Conflict
Twin sisters, Mazie and Daisy wear each other's clothes without regard for cleaning and returning them to the other.	Daisy sneaks into Mazie's room as soon as she leaves for work and picks a brand-new dress to wear. Mazie installs a deadbolt lock on her bedroom door. (destructive complementarity).	Mazie begins to feel bad about the way she treats her sister's things and apologizes. Daisy apologizes as well when she takes a moment to empathize and understand that their relationship is important. (constructive symmetry).

MANAGING INTERPERSONAL CONFLICT

Interpersonal conflict can either be

- Functional that can be beneficial for a relationship because it provides a way for individuals to solve problems and improve communication.
- Dysfunctional that is harmful because it can ultimately weaken relationships.

Whether a conflict is functional or dysfunctional relies in part on the methods we choose to resolve them.

While managing conflicts depends on many factors including one's general attitude toward conflict, perceptions of the issues and reaction to power, there are a host of models, strategies, tactics, and techniques that can be beneficial.

If Bryant and his parents are feeling pressure because of having to make a decision about which college Bryant will attend, it seems unlikely they will have consensus on the issue. They may experience increasing stress as tensions build. How they choose to respond to each other can either escalate or deescalate the conflict. They would do well to remember: you can win the battle, but ultimately lose the war.

POWER IN CONFLICT SITUATIONS

Types of Authority or Status or Power

Power is a central feature in most conflict situations. Interpersonal power is the degree to which a person is able to influence or control another. So, person A has power over person B when A can influence or control B's behavior.

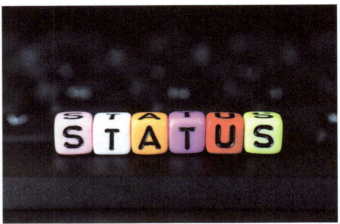

However, it is not simply one person pulling the strings of another like a puppet. Power doesn't necessarily reside in people, it is negotiated between individuals. It is through communication that a measure of mutual influence (power) is realized. We allow others to influence us and we in turn influence them.

Consider our earlier example of the conflict between Bryant and his parents. It is clear that the ultimate decision rests with his parents because they have to give their approval since Bryant is still underage. In such dependent relationships, a person will have a greater need for the other to realize their goals and therefore power tends to be out of balance (parents have more power than a child).

Power depends on the individual and circumstances. When needs change, power and influence can change (when a child reaches adulthood, parents have less power). We can only have power when the other is willing to accept our power.

Since the clear majority of conflicts occur between individuals who are in relationship, there are different types of power that individuals use in conflict situations:

Legitimate Power

You have this power or you perceive others have it by virtue of the position you or others hold.

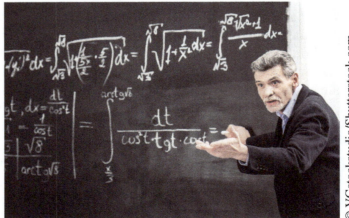

- Parents have legitimate power in the home.
- Professors have legitimate power in the classroom.
- Your boss has legitimate power in the workplace.

Expert Power

You hold this power or you perceive others do because you or they know things others don't.

Or, you give this power to others because they have information you need. Your professors have expert power in the classroom. When your professor comes into your workplace asking for help, you have the expert power.

The architect in this photograph has power in your building relationship because you need your house to meet the building codes.

© Rawpixel.com/Shutterstock.com

Referent Power

You hold this power because you are a role model for someone. Or, you give someone this power because you see that person as a role model.

This power is used by advertisers to sell products. The use of a star athlete, Hollywood A-lister or D-lister for that matter, a rock or rap star or one of the Kardashians in a commercial is an example of referent power.

Of course, you could see your older sibling as a role model.

© CREATISTA/Shutterstock.com

Reward Power

This power is held by you if you can reward someone or by another if you perceive that person can reward you.

A parent with a cookie or later a car, a boss with a raise, or a professor with an "A," are examples of this type of power.

That's the carrot part. The stick part is

© ChameleonsEye/Shutterstock.com

Coercive Power

This power uses punishment, physical, emotional, psychological, and material to exert power.

You did this when you were little and threatened your parents that you would hold your breath until you passed out if you did not get a cookie. Your parents replied with the coercive power of spanking.

Your boss tried to coerce you into an inappropriate relationship. You try that on your boss and it is also coercive power.

© ChameleonsEye/Shutterstock.com

Information or Persuasive Power

You exercise this power when you convince your friends that you all really want to see Batman versus Superman (28% on the Tomato Meter) rather than Jason Bourne (56% on the Tomato Meter).

You give this power to your friends when you decide to be persuaded by them that the Denver Airport Conspiracy Theory is true.

© lexaarts/Shutterstock.com

S-TLC SYSTEM

One model designed to help us manage basic communication skills is the S-TLC system, developed by Cahn and Abigail (2007). The S-TLC system is an acronym for Stop, Think, Listen, and Communicate.

© Profit_Image/Shutterstock.com

Stop

- Tell yourself to "stop"—take time out.
- Exit temporarily if necessary to get hold of yourself.
- Count to 100 or begin to breathe deeply to calm yourself down.

© Archiwiz/Shutterstock.com

Think

- Think before you act or talk.
- Try not to take things personally.
- Avoid jumping to conclusions.

© Ollyy/Shutterstock.com

Think about your options and ask yourself: "What do I want to accomplish?"

Think both about the problem and about your relationship with the other person.

Listen

Listen before you say anything. The tendency of most people is to justify themselves the moment they hear criticism—instead try to listen mindfully to what the other person is saying.

Listening mindfully is a way to affirm the value and worth of others.

Consider this . . . the feeling of being truly heard is so close to the feeling of being loved that most people cannot tell the difference!!!

© Antonio Guillem/Shutterstock.com

Communicate

Decide in **advance** how you want to communicate—we can choose our communicative behavior.

Try to choose responses that will not escalate the conflict—but move you toward mutual satisfaction and collaboration.

© Belinda Pretorius/Shutterstock.com

Critical Thinking Exercise:

YouTube URL: http://www.youtube.com/watch?v=6xCkhV7zhuw

TedTalk by Dr. William Ury

We all face conflict from time to time. If you are human and you interact with other humans, there is always the possibility of experiencing differences.

In this very interesting TedTalk, William Ury offers a solution that is amazing in its simplicity. While he poses a very simple question—***How do we deal with our human differences?*** —it's really the answers he provides that lay a framework for solutions that any one of us can use in managing our relationships.

Prior to a class discussion, briefly respond to the following questions after viewing the TedTalk by William Ury.

1) Explain the "secret to peace" that Dr. Ury outlines in this message.
2) Who is the "third side" and would you consider them important to resolving conflict? What would you consider the role of the third side?
3) What are the implications of Dr. Ury's suggestions for your own relationships?

Chapter 10

"I Love You." "I know."

—Princess Leia and Han Solo, *The Empire Strikes Back*

A Discussion of Relationships

© ESB Professional/Shutterstock.com

Chapter 1 told you that Communication is the relationship. You can't have a relationship with someone unless you are communicating with that person in some way. Those involved in the relationship make the choice of how, how much, and when they will communicate. Those decisions will reflect what kind of relationship you have with these people and how you want to express that relationship.

- You have people you consider friends you talk to occasionally.
- You have friends you see and interact with every day.
- You may have a friend who contacts you only on your birthday or at holiday time but the two of you still consider yourselves friends.

It's not the quantity of communication that is important. It's the quality. For example, couples who talk about important topics and do it well are more satisfied with their relationship than couples who talk minimally to each other. However, when a couple, whether that is a friendship or romantic couple, have been together for a long time, the need to talk diminishes. The communication is nonverbal and exists as a confirmation that the couple is confident and secure in the relationship. No verbal communication is necessary.

The important thing to remember is that you cannot be in a relationship with someone you are not communicating with. The type and amount of communication is your choice. But the communication must be happening or there is no relationship.

An argument can be made that a relationship can also exist with a higher power.

As always, we will start with a definition so we all know what we are talking about.

Relationships are: associations between two or more people who are interdependent, who use some consistent patterns of interaction, and who have interacted for a period of time. (Pearson and Nelson 2007).

As you read through this chapter, you are likely to filter all the information through your romantic relationships. That's fine. However, everything discussed in this chapter is applicable to every relationship you have.

Relationships are measured on a continuum or scale of level of intimacy.

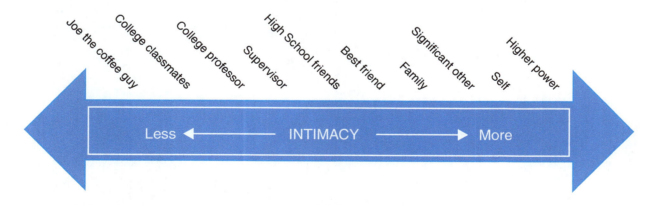

You will be less intimate with people such as "Joe the coffee guy" whom you may see each morning when you stop for coffee on the way to school or work. Your communication with Joe would be limited to small talk. Now, compare that to a conversation with your significant other, which would be on a much deeper and more intimate level. It might sound odd to say you would communicate with "self" but, we do talk to ourselves, mostly internally, when we are trying to weigh decision-making options, when we want to encourage ourselves and sadly, when we tell ourselves that we are not going to be successful at something such as giving a speech.

Understanding, respecting, and effectively communicating with people according to level of intimacy demonstrates interpersonal communication competency. For example, the way you greet your professor or boss is not the same way you greet your BFF or significant other. Surprisingly, not everyone realizes that.

Let's look at some different types of relationships and interactions more closely. We will do this by breaking down the definition.

Associations between two or more people—

■ Romantic Couple
■ Best Friend
■ Teacher and Student
■ Teacher and Class
■ Family Unit
■ Friendship Group
■ Co-workers

These associations can run the gamut from being intimate like a romantic couple to friendship like this young woman and her little friend to barely knowing someone like the person you see every day on the bus ride to class or "Joe the coffee guy". The point is that you interact with these people. You communicate with them. You agree to be together.

Interdependent People

A relationship exists if you are mutually dependent with a person and each person has an impact on the other. You need each other. That need is different for different relationships, but the need is there. More importantly, you are responsible for each other.

Once you decide to be in relationship with someone, you have responsibilities for and obligations to that person. Part of building and maintaining your relationship is the communication you have about what those responsibilities and obligations are.

Let's use a friend as an example. You decide to be friends with someone who lives far away. The rules for the friendship need to take that into account. You two decide that you will call one another once a week, communicate (text, Instagram, Snapchat, Facebook) on each other's birthdays, and meet up once a year. Those are the obligations. The responsibility is to carry out this program.

Consistent Patterns of Interaction

Relationships need stability and predictability, although later in the chapter we will discuss the need for novelty in relationships. People in relationships need to feel secure. They need to know that there will be a routine. That routine includes typical things like

- leaving for the day and returning
- reactions to behaviors
- weekend activities

We develop behaviors within relationship to shore them up.

- We make up family nicknames.
- We greet our friends perhaps with a handshake developed just for that friendship.
- We say hello to the bus driver every morning.

These behaviors assure people that the relationship is ongoing. The behaviors reassure each person in the relationship that everything is fine. When these interactions change, people know that something is up.

Interaction over a Period of Time

On-off interactions do not make a relationship.

While you might form an instant liking for another person, you are not yet in relationship with that person.

It is not possible to develop consistent patterns of interaction if you do not take the time to work out what those will be. A one night stand is not a relationship.

HERE IS ONE OF MY RELATIONSHIPS

Using the definition as an outline, analyze one relationship you have.

Association of two or more people:

Interdependent: (How are you interdependent with these others?)

Consistent Pattern of Interactions: (List some)

Time: (How long has this been going on?)

WHAT IS SO IMPORTANT ABOUT INTERPERSONAL RELATIONSHIPS?

Who taught you math? How did you learn to drive? When did you realize you were a good athlete? How were you introduced to your first instrument? How did you develop your moral code? You know the answers to these questions and you know those answers involve other people. It is, in fact, all about the relationship.

John Donne was right when he said, "no man is an island". In the meditation in which this phrase is found, Donne argues that all people are connected, that we need others. How right he was. Relationships are necessary because through them we

© ESB Professional/Shutterstock.com

Come to Understand Ourselves

Generally, you trust the people with whom you have close relationships. You are willing to listen to their assessments of you and integrate them into your understanding of yourself if you find those assessments useful.

You can find out about yourself by yourself but how much more fun is it to learn about who you are together with people you trust.

© igorstevanovic/Shutterstock.com

Come to Understand Others

We have preconceived notions about people. Relationships help us to analyze these notions and decide if they are accurate.

The more we know others, the more likely we are to communicate well with them. We know the audience, so to speak, and can tailor the message to that audience. For example, many of our elderly grew up with the understanding that people should be addressed by title and last name until told otherwise. You know this about your elderly neighbor and so use that form of address.

© VGstockstudio/Shutterstock.com

Come to Understand the World

We learn about the world around us through the relationships we have.

Who formed your opinions about life? Your morals? Who taught you to read, do math? Most likely someone you were in relationship with introduced you to these things. Some children can learn to read and do math on their own. Even so, the materials they use to read and do math are brought to them by people with whom they are in a relationship.

225 FLAGS OF THE WORLD

© Musheg Mkhitaryan/Shutterstock.com

Cope with Life

The home is a place to rest. It is supposed to be a place of security from the outside world. We return to a place of safety, whether it is a home or some other place we have designed for that purpose so that we can rest and recharge.

Friends or intimates help us cope with the pressures and stresses of life. Even acquaintances like a bartender or hairdresser can be that help.

Relationships help you stay in college. The people who have friends, mentors, and others who care, are more likely to stay in college and complete a degree.

© William Perugini/Shutterstock.com

Fulfill Needs

You have probably seen this pyramid before. It is based on Abraham Maslow's Hierarchy of Needs. The pyramid illustrates five levels of needs all human beings have.

You will find relationships that meet these needs for you. That is one reason why some people have many different types of relationships. No one person can meet every need. And if you don't believe that or think that should not be true, look at this list of needs:

Basic human Needs

Self Actualization
Self Esteem
Love and Belonging
Safe and Security
Basic Physioloyical

© Rawpixel.com/Shutterstock.com

- Spiritual Needs—the need for transcendence
- Social Needs—the need to be with people and be liked and accepted
- Intellectual Needs—the need to appear smart. The need to exercise your brain
- Physical—the need to move, participate in activities, sex
- Emotional—the need to feel loved and belong
- Security—the need to feel safe
- Biological—the need to eat, sleep, and breathe

And then argue that one person can meet all of these, all the time.

Increase and Enrich Our Experiences

© Rawpixel.com/Shutterstock.com

How much of your family history do you know? What have your grandparents told you that makes a difference in your life?

Do you have friends who are always dragging you out to do things you normally would not do like, say, bowling? Did you find you liked it? That you learned something new? That at least you had a story to tell after the bowling experience to amuse others with?

And while it can be delightful being out and about by yourself, sharing an experience with another, especially another you are close to, has greater rewards.

MY BEST FRIEND

Fill in the blanks about your relationship with your best friend. What has your best friend done for you?

Understand myself:

Understand my best friend:

Understand the world:

Cope with tough stuff:

Meet needs:

WHAT'S UP WITH MILLENNIALS?

If you are between the ages of 18 and 35 you are a Millennial. You are part of the biggest generation with 85–90 million of you populating the planet. One of the perks of being a Millennial is that researchers are now seeking you out to study you in all sorts of ways. Naturally, one of those ways is relationships. So, what is the skinny on how Millennials relate to one another?

Much of your relationship interaction is done online.

- Video gaming
- Online role-playing
- Texting
- Snapchat
- Tumblr

© Eugenio Marongiu/Shutterstock.com

- Tinder
- Facebook

© oneinchpunch/Shutterstock.com

Your friendships are often carried out online. In fact, you have to do this as you are not getting driver's licenses. Uber and urban living have something to do with the decline in driving, but the focus on online relationships also plays a part. Look at this picture. What does it tell you?

It tells you that even when you are together you are on your phone not talking to the people around you. Do you find this true in your own life?

When it comes to romantic relationships Millennials are more open to variety but are also more anxious about success and stability. Many of you are from divorced households and so find romance and marriage as a scary thing.

Your views on marriage are interesting. Look at this chart (Time, 2017). It is a distillation of a survey that tracks the millennial view of marriage. The survey asked Millennials, which of these marriage models they would be interested in using. Here are the answers:

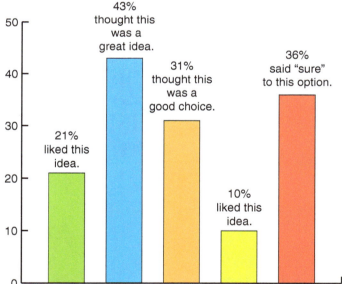

(Time, 2017)

- 43% thought this was a great idea.
- 31% thought this was a good choice.
- 36% said "sure" to this option.
- 21% liked this idea.
- 10% liked this idea.

The Presidential Model: Vows last for four years, then another four years. After eight years you can choose a new partner.

Beta Model: The union can be formalized or dissolved after two years.

'Til Death Do Us Part Model: Divorce is illegal

Multiple Partner Model: You can be married to more than one person at a time, with each fulfilling a need for you

Real Estate Model: A marriage license is good for 5,7,10 and 30 years. At the end of these times the marriage must be renegotiated and another license issued.

Part of the relational anxiety reported by Millennials stems from

The Peter Pan Problem

As its name implies, this problem comes from not wanting or feeling the need to grow up. Studies show that Millennials don't consider themselves grown up until they are 30. Some don't believe they are grown up until 40. Take this quote of example:

Even our vocabulary reveals our disdain for growing up. "Adulting" is a versatile verb we use to describe boring or responsibility-laden activities, such as paying taxes, cooking dinner, or even doing laundry (since apparently kids don't do laundry). It's our way of saying that growing up is an undesirable thing to have to do. (Snow, 2016)

Casual or even intense friendships can probably survive perpetual adolescence, but romantic relationships can't.

The FOBO Problem

FOBO stands for Fear of Better Options, a phrase coined by Priya Parker, who is an expert-in-residence at the Harvard Innovation Lab. There was a time when your friend and romantic options were quite limited. Your family's social circle, your place of worship, your school, and your work were about it. With limited options, you would choose the best people available for friends and then look for the best fit for a romantic partner. This is no longer true. With access to the world through the Internet, you have or at least you think you have unlimited options. Hence FOBO. If you are waiting for "the right one" or anxious over "the one that got away," you are likely to never make a choice.

The Economic Problem

Millennial college graduates carry a significant amount of debt. There is credit card debt. There is student loan debt. There is car loan debt. Such debts can amount to a monthly mortgage payment, which you cannot make because you are trying to pay off student loan, car, and credit card debt.

Heavy debt makes you less interesting as a romantic partner. It certainly makes it difficult for couples to budget when both are saddled with debt coming into the relationship.

This problem is compounded by low paying jobs or no job after graduation.

Despite what you have heard, it is not sex that causes most fights in romantic relationships. It's money.

The Online Dating Problem

According to Pew Research, one in five adults between 25–34 years old has used online dating. And why not. Millennials live much of their lives online.

And there is so much to choose from. You would not know it from the commercials you hear, but here are more than 2,500 online dating services in the United States. There are services that target Millennials. These are for example,

Tinder. A fun fact: 90% of Tinder-users, are between ages 18 and 34.

Hinge

Bumble

So, what is the problem? People lie on their profiles. Because of lying, most people never meet face-to-face. The FOBO problem comes into play here as well.

The Texting Problem

Texting allows for fewer face-to-face encounters.

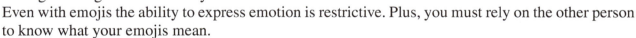

It also makes you lazy in your relationships. There is no need to meet someone for a walk or a dinner when you can sit in the comfort of your house and chat with them via text.

The problem is that the fewer face-to-face interactions you have with the person you are in relationship with, the smaller the investment in the relationship both of you have. It is much easier to walk away from a relationship in which you have invested so little.

Then there is the problem of the limits of texting. Texting does not convey emotions well. Even with emojis the ability to express emotion is restrictive. Plus, you must rely on the other person to know what your emojis mean.

It is easier to be mean and cruel via text. Have you even broken up with or been broken up via text? How did that make you feel?

It is no surprise then that 40% of Millennials believe that dating is harder now than it was for their parents and grandparents. (pewsocialtrends, 2014) 8 in 10 Millennials say that true romance is very important. Pew also noted that 61% of Millennials would like to marry someday. Millennials want lasting relationships.

There are no easy answers to these problems. There are a few things to learn that can help. Here they are.

WHY ARE YOU ATTRACTED TO SOME PEOPLE AND NOT OTHERS?

It's true, of course. You find some people attractive and some not. You want to get to know some people and not others. You want to date some people and not others. You want to be friends with some people and not others. There are reasons why this is true. And now you want to know what those reasons are. Here then.

© marekuliasz/Shutterstock.com

Attraction Theory

This theory suggests that people are attracted to each other for a variety of different reasons. Those reasons could be based on attractiveness, proximity, similarity, or complementarily.

© Olivier Le Moal/Shutterstock.com

Physical Attraction

You are attracted to a particular physical type. While it is not true for everyone, most people have a "type" they prefer.

Some people want to date people more attractive than themselves. Others want to date people equally as attractive. Still others want to date those less attractive than themselves.

All this is to say that attractiveness count. Even though you have been told for as long as you can remember that it's what's inside that

© kurhan/Shutterstock.com

counts you are unlikely to even approach a person who is not physically attractive to you in some way.

Those constructs we talked about in the Perception chapter come into play here. You have a vision of the type of person who is most attractive to you. You will look for that.

The down side of this is that you may pass by someone you could really connect with because that person is not your physical type.

Personal Attributes Attraction

Certain people have a gift that makes them beautiful to others regardless of their physical characteristics. These people, by the force of their personalities, are attractive to others.

In cultures where humor is highly prized, a person who is charming and funny is seen as attractive.

Kind people have the same thing going for them.

© serato/Shutterstock.com

Perceived Competence Attraction

You are attracted to people you believe to be competent (McCloskey and McCain, 1974). This competence shows itself in what people do.

© marekuliasz/Shutterstock.com

- A great singer or rapper
- A good cook
- A strong dancer
- A brilliant craftsperson
- A talented computer geek

Or these accomplished aikido masters practicing their technique.

Some of our recent hunky male action stars are not conventionally attractive, but they are competent. These guys become attractive to us because their competence makes them more physically appealing. Who are we talking about here? For *Terminator* fans, we are talking Arnold Schwarzenegger. Who else?

Have you noticed that the hero's sidekick in movies these days is often the nerdy techie? Sometimes this person is conventionally attractive. Often, this person is quirky in some way. But these characters scream competence. We are attracted to them because of that competence.

These people attract us because we want to be around successful, creative people. Some of your friendships are based on this kind of attraction. And clearly, you will choose a romantic interest with this attraction in the mix.

RE-ENFORCEMENT OR REWARD THEORY

Reward Theory as its name implies, suggests that you are in relationship with people who can reward you in some way. The "reward" is a perception that you hold. You make the decision about what constitutes a reward. That reward may look small to those around you, but if it is important to you will maintain a relationship to get it.

I have two words for you: Trophy Wife. The Trophy Wife relationship is a reward-based one. The young, often beautiful wife rewards the older husband with beauty, elegance, perhaps a child and the older husband rewards the wife with money and security. You will decide for yourself whether you think this is OK.

Reward Theory extends to business as well. You may stay at a job because of the rewards that job offers you.

You may have friends you don't particularly like, but you maintain that friendship because those friends can get you things you want.

© sondem/Shutterstock.com

PROXIMITY THEORY

This theory suggests that we become attracted to people who are in our general orbit day in and day out. These are the people we

- go to class with
- work with
- are friends of friends
- ride the bus with
- see every time we go to our favorite café

© Naga Venkatesh Sankar R/Shutterstock.com

These may be the people you text every day and so know them that way even if you have never met face-to-face.

Proximity was the classic way people used to meet. Prior to the open-ended Internet, your choice of a friend or romantic partner was limited to the people nearest you. That's always providing you were not a mail-order bride or the gentleman who purchased that mail order.

Proximity is the idea behind arranged marriages. Parents will arrange the marriage of their children to those in the same village or social circle. The point of such a marriage is the merger of two families. The marriage enhances the families' fortunes so it is important to have some connection—perhaps adjoining farms or businesses.

In most states, it is legal for employers to forbid employee dating. Bummer. After all, if we meet and get to know and are attracted to people through proximity what better place to do that than at work. And employers do take this option. So, let's debate:

THE GREAT DEBATE

Resolved: Employers should prohibit dating among employees

The class will be divided into debate teams. You will have 10 minutes to search the Internet for information to defend both the affirmative and the negative of this resolution. Then you will debate.

Affirmative (Yes, employers should ban dating.)

Negative (No, employers should not ban dating.)

SIMILARITY THEORY

Obviously, you are attracted to people who are like you. Being attracted to people like us validates who we are. It re-enforces our beliefs, attitudes, values, and behaviors.

The similarity can be as obvious, as with our French bulldog here, as looking alike.

But similarity also extends to

- Politics
- Music
- Fashion
- Sports
- Fandom of any kind
- Religion
- Education

There is a certain strain of confirmation bias at play here. You surround yourself with people who think like you and that helps you feel comfortable about how you view the world.

The bottom line of similarity is that you build up what you already have in the relationships you form.

- You are an SU basketball fan so you have SU basketball fan friends.
- You rap so you have rapper friends.
- You have a degree in Economics so your significant other also has one.

What is the upside of this attraction?

What is the downside of this attraction?

COMPLEMENTARY THEORY

People who are dissimilar are often attracted to each other. These are the relationships about which the questions are asked,

"What do they see in each other?" and

"How do they get along?"

A classic example of this type of relationship is the power couple Mary Matalin and James Carville.

They married in 1993 to the amazement of Washington, D.C. Ms. Matalin is a Republican and worked for the George W. Bush campaign. Mr. Carville is a Democrat and is a Clinton loyalist. How do they manage this vast difference? For one thing, they don't talk politics at home.

The attraction in a complementary relationship is the added bonus. Rather than building up what you already have (similarity), this attraction adds to who you are and what you know.

The same list that you saw above for Similarity applies here.

- You like Country music and your significant other likes classic rock.
- You prefer horror movies and your friend prefers comedy.
- You love Harry Potter and your friend can't even get through the first 20 pages.
- Star Wars versus Star Trek.

What is the upside of this attraction?

What is the downside of this attraction?

COST/BENEFITS THEORY

There are several theories, which suggest that relationships are built and maintained or terminated based on a cost/ benefits analysis. You stay in a relationship when the benefits outweigh the costs and leave if the costs become too much.

© Olivier Le Moal/Shutterstock.com

Another consideration is equity. You hope that the relationship will be equitable in how the costs and rewards are divided up. Is a relationship worth the trouble if the other person is getting more out of it than you are?

Your idea of expectations (remember the Perception chapter?) are in play here. You have expectations of what a friendship should be. Or, a romantic relationship for that matter. What beliefs, attitudes, values, and behaviors do you expect in a friendship? A romantic relationship? Met expectations (remembering a birthday, spending time together) are rewards/benefits. Unmet expectations are costs.

Military spouses face significant costs in their relationships with their partners. Expectations say that married couples spend a lot of time together. Not so with military marrieds. Military marrieds are often separated for long periods of time with minimal contact during that separation. If this cost becomes too great, the marriage will not survive.

You may have at some time begged a friend, a sibling, or a parent to get out of a relationship you thought was unhealthy. You couldn't get that person to listen to you. Cost/Benefit Theory is why. Only the person knows what is a benefit and what is a cost. Only the person knows how much to put up with for the sake of the relationship. The person must make the decision that the costs have become too great.

TYPES OF RELATIONSHIPS

Relationships are not all the same. They come in a wide variety of types. In order to build and maintain good relationships, you need to know what kind of relationship you are in. You need to know how to judge, when to move to the next level, or when to call it quits.

© Gustavo Frazao/Shutterstock.com

You decide where you want your relationship to go, with the other person in mind of course.

Here are the types of relationships you can have. They are not mutually exclusive. You can move in and out of them.

Acquaintance

These are people you barely know. You run into them every day, but your contact is superficial.

You probably know very little about these people, not even a name.

You most likely discuss the weather or the sports news, while staying away from touchy subjects like politics or social issues.

Examples of acquaintance relationships are:

- Secretaries
- Bus drivers
- Your barista

Such relationships can blossom into real friendships. After all, we all start out as acquaintance. If you decide you want a friendship with an acquaintance, you begin the task of self-disclosure. You start probing to see if this person wants more of a relationship.

Friends

Friendships come in a variety of shapes and sizes. The variety is wide because friends meet different needs for us. You may have

- Movie friends
- Coffee friends
- Sports friends
- Lunch friends
- Dinner friends
- BFF
- Family friends

These titles mean different things. You have friends you do everything with and friends you barely talk to. You have friends you may not like (see Reward Theory) and friends who are closer to you than your siblings.

Good friendships take time and energy to pursue. That's why it is so difficult to maintain many close friendships. There simply isn't time.

Perhaps we should address Facebook, Snapchat, Instagram, and Twitter in this regard. These people are not your friends. Unless you have known someone for a long time and are actually in relationship with them, people who friend you in these venues are not "friends" in any meaningful way. They do not go out to dinner with you, have coffee with you, go to class with you, visit you in the hospital, keep your secrets, or do any of the things live-person friends do.

Intimate

These relationships are special. You have them one at a time. They require a deep level of all the communication behaviors we have discussed so far.

These relationships are important, so much so that much of music, literature, movies, and life are centered around them.

Think about the movies and TV shows you watch and the music that you listen to. The chief driver of conflict in these bits of entertainment is intimate relationships.

© Lightspring/Shutterstock.com

- The first John Wick movie is kickstarted when his new puppy, a parting gift from his dying wife, is killed by deranged gangsters. He kills about 45 people as a result. It's a classic revenge film.
- Snape has an unrequited love for Harry's mother, which explains his behaviors.
- Titanic.

Undoubtedly, intimate relationships are important. They are also risky. It is in intimate relationships that you self-disclose with abandon. These relationships require trust at a level not reached in other types of relationships.

Role

This relationship is supposed to be unambiguous. You both know why you are there and you know the relationship is purely professional. Each of you have a role to play in this relationship and you know what it is.

This Physical Therapist (PT) is doing stretching exercises on a patient. The PT is touching the patient in a professional manner, which is wholly appropriate for this relationship.

Examples of role relationships are:

© Dmytro Zinkevych/Shutterstock.com

- Doctor with patient;
- Teacher and student;
- Sale clerk with customer.

The difficulty comes when you have not made it clear which level you are on. Self-disclosure rules should help here, but they do not always do so. You also should make clear what you expect from a person on a given level. People have different ideas or expectations about relationships. Men and women have this problem when it comes to the intimate level. What is your definition of intimacy? It makes a difference.

SHOULD PROFESSORS DATE THEIR STUDENTS?

The professor/student relationship is a role relationship. Role relationships, like other relationships, have rules to follow.

In your opinion, what are the rules for a professor/student relationship?

Should professors date their students? Defend your answer.

POWER IN RELATIONSHIPS

Since we just discussed whether professors and students should date, we should probably move on to how authority, status, and power work in relationships. Authority, status, and power are part of every relationship. They are not, however, consistent elements as they vary due to context and a couple of other factors, which we will discuss below.

Authority or status or power in relationships is derived from the following characteristics, although it's not limited to these:

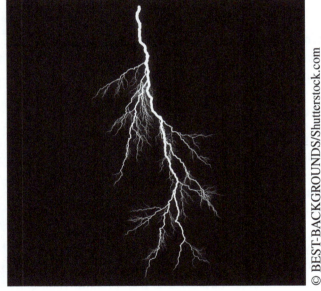

© BEST-BACKGROUNDS/Shutterstock.com

- Economic status
- Athletic ability
- Body shape and weight
- Family background
- Age
- Knowledge or wisdom
- Confidence

These characteristics are highly influenced by culture. Cultures are classified along a continuum of High Power Distance to Low Power Distance in how power is perceived and used in relationships.

High Power Distance cultures have these characteristics.

- A wide divide between the powerful and the powerless.
- Authority and power is expected and considered desirable.
- Class is important. Authority or status or power is inherited.
- Reliance on power symbols like titles, offices, and material goods.
- A few at the top have most of the power. The vast majority of the culture has none.
- Friendships are class-based.
- Deference is expected to those with power.
- Examples: Mexico, Brazil, and Philippines.

© javarman/Shutterstock.com

Low Power Distance cultures have these characteristics.

- Authority is questioned.
- Authority or status or power can be earned.
- Power is spread among more people.
- Friendships cross class lines.
- Class is not a defining feature; therefore, people can move up and down the class structure.
- Assertiveness is expected.
- Symbols of authority or status or power have less importance.
- Examples: Denmark and Sweden.

© Gertjan Hooijer/Shutterstock.com

VERBAL COMMUNICATION

Authority or status or power is telegraphed by how you use language. The more confidently you use language, the more authority you will hold. Powerful talk enhances your ability to communicate. Powerless talk makes you appear weak.

© Phovoir/Shutterstock.com

Powerful talk includes

- A large vocabulary.
- Correct pronunciation.
- Correct use of words. You really should know the definition of a word before you use it.
- The ability to "sound like" your listener.

© vitasunny/Shutterstock.com

Powerless talk includes

- Hesitations:
  - ❏ um, uh,
  - ❏ you know,
  - ❏ just really.

© nnattalli/Shutterstock.com

- Over-use of Intensifiers:
  - ❏ truly,
  - ❏ best ever,
  - ❏ always,
  - ❏ never.

- Disqualifiers:
  - ❏ "I didn't read the book but. . ."
  - ❏ "I didn't actually hear this said, but. . ."
  - ❏ "I didn't see the movie, but. . ."

- Disclaimers:
  - ❏ "You probably don't want to hear this, but. . ."
  - ❏ "Don't be mad, but. . ."
  - ❏ "Promise you won't tell, but. . ."

- Tag questions:
  - ❏ "You understand what I am saying?"
  - ❏ "You know what I mean?"
  - ❏ "Got that?"

- Self-critical statements:
  - ❏ "This isn't my specialty, but. . ."
  - ❏ "I am not good at this, but. . ."
  - ❏ "I know I am not smart about these things. . ."

Some of this powerless talk sounds like whining. Some of it sounds like you think others aren't smart enough to understand you. Some of it sounds like you don't know what you want to say next. All of it can be annoying if done repeatedly in a conversation. All of it strips you of authority or status or power.

NONVERBAL COMMUNICATION

© sportpoint/Shutterstock.com

Authority or status or power is conveyed nonverbally as well. How is this accomplished?

Body shape and weight.

In some cultures, it is "the big man," the man who, in the United States would be considered overweight, who has the most authority or status or power.

In the United States, it is low-weight women who are considered attractive and therefore powerful.

Does this man project authority or status or power? If you think so, why do you think that?

© Vladimir Gjorgiev/Shutterstock.com

Clothing

Expensive clothes are powerful. Cheap clothes are not.

You remember in "Silence of the Lambs," Hannibal Lecter exerts power over Clarice Starling by making fun of her designer knock-off shoes.

Sophistication is powerful. The power couple in the photo are wearing expensive clothes. The clothing telegraphs that they have money (even if that isn't the reality.) They can probably cut the line at a club and double park without getting a ticket.

Cutesy is powerless because it makes you seem like a child. That is true for both men and women.

Dressing like a teen when you are over 40 is considered powerless.

Take a look at the newest trend in men's summer wear, the RompHim™

https://www.kickstarter.com/projects/106904571/the-romphimtm-your-new-favorite-summer-outfit

© Sundraw Photography/Shutterstock.com

Trendy is powerless as it shows you are easily lead. Style is powerful as it shows you have your own mind.

Fashion says, me, too. Style says, only me.

Territory

You feel more powerful in your own space because you can control it.

You design your space to show your power. A big corner office with windows shows you are the boss. A little cubicle shows you are a minion.

© Breadmaker/Shutterstock.com

LESS IS MORE

Less is more when assessing authority or status or power in relationships. Generally speaking, the less interested a person is in the relationship the more power that person has. It is the person who craves the relationship who will do anything to maintain it. Think of the bully with a toady who does errands and takes abuse from the bully.

The more you need the relationship, the less power you have. The golden handcuffs keep you in a job you do not want because you need what those handcuffs provide.

© Sokolova23/Shutterstock.com

The more powerful you are, the less interested you are in rewards and punishment. You can easily leave a relationship because you have somewhere to go. Punishment doesn't mean much if you can take the sting out of that punishment.

YOUR CHOICE OF RELATIONSHIP

In your friendships and in your romantic relationships, you should decide how power will be distributed. Those in the relationship can decide on having a symmetrical or complementary power relationship.

© EtiAmmos/Shutterstock.com

Symmetrical

The symmetrical power relationship works in a couple of different ways.

- You can agree who is in control but not abide by that agreement.
- Power is constantly challenged when someone exercises it.
- One person abdicates power but the other does not pick it up, so there is a power vacuum.
- Power changes with each situation. The person most likely to have, let's say the knowledge, is the one with the power.

People in symmetrical relationships can feel good about them because each person can exercise power. Symmetrical relationships can be a problem when neither one of the participants wants power or when one is constantly abdicating the agreed upon responsibility to exercise power.

Complementary

People in complementary relationships do not share power. One person either assumes all the power or one person gives all the power to the other.

Power does not change no matter who has more knowledge or is better able to offer rewards.

Such relationships have the advantage of having a "go to" person for all major decisions. Stability in decision-making seems to be a priority in such relationships. The downside of complementary relationships is not having the best person available making the decisions.

LEVELS OF COMMUNICATION WITHIN RELATIONSHIPS

One of the ways you know what level of relationship you are on with a person is the way you communicate with that person. Relationships can have big problems if one of you is communicating on a level not shared or wanted by the other.

Here are the levels of communication. See if you can fit them into the levels of relationship.

Small Talk

You know what small talk is. It is superficial communication, which consists mainly of acknowledging the existence of the other. It is not intended to reveal or share ideas and feelings.

Generally, small talk is used to meet social expectations when chatting up acquaintances.

When engaging in small talk with friends, you are in a sense building your relationship. Not every communication you have with friends has to be deep and serious. Small talk functions as a way to enjoy one another's company without having to expend too much energy.

Small talk is a staple of social situations. Avoiding difficult topics such as politics, social issues, and religion keeps social situations such as parties and dinners fun and relaxed.

Gossip

When you hear the word "gossip" do you think of chatting about people and saying nice things about them? Probably not. Gossip is usually associated with making negative comments about another.

Gossip is "talking about others." That talking usually means saying something negative about another.

Gossip is a slightly higher level of communication than small talk because you are in fact revealing something about yourself. It is one thing to reveal in small talk that you like Kanye West. It's another entirely to reveal that you are willing to say unkind, unverifiable things about your friends. What you reveal about yourself is that you are not kind nor are you trustworthy.

Celebrity gossip is technically gossip, but it is closer to small talk than actual gossip. We like to gossip about celebrities and because we don't know them personally, this gossip seems to be harmless.

Gossip about friends and family is entirely different. This kind of gossip can be hurtful.

Exchanging Ideas, Beliefs, Attitudes, and Values

Once you decide you want to exchange more than pleasantries with people, your communication rises to the level of ideas, beliefs, attitudes, and values exchange.

Now, you are revealing things about yourself and the communication becomes riskier.

Even if you know someone well, you can't be sure how your ideas, beliefs, attitudes, and values will be received.

For example, your idea of how to make politics in Washington work better is to require by law all Congressional Representatives to come to work every day dressed as their state's official animal. In the case of the representatives from New York, all would be dressed as beavers. Now, you might think this is really funny. But for people for whom politics is deadly serious stuff, this "idea exchange" will not, trust me, be funny.

Sharing Deep Feelings

You share deep feelings with very few people. Usually this level of communication is confined to intimate friends or romantic couples.

This is where you reveal a lot about yourself and you won't do it for just anyone.

Self-disclosure is at its peak at this level of communication.

© nd3000/Shutterstock.com

ELEMENTS OF SATISFYING PERSONAL RELATIONSHIPS

You want your relationships to be successful and satisfying. It doesn't matter if that relationship is a friendship, an acquaintance, a co-worker, or a romantic partner you want it to work or you would not be in it. Successful and satisfying relationships are possible, but they take time and effort. They take investment, commitment, and trust.

© asife/Shutterstock.com

Investment

Investment in a relationship is what we put into the relationship that we cannot get back if the relationship fails.

- Time
- Material Goods
- Energy

You and the people you are in relationship with make decisions about how much you will invest

© TZIDO SUN/Shutterstock.com

each of these elements in that relationship. Everyone in the relationship needs to be on board with these choices.

How much money should you spend for a gift in the following relationships:
- An office holiday gift exchange: _____
- A new romantic interest's birthday: _____
- Your BFF's birthday: _____

You are in a romantic relationship. How much time do you think you should spend together?
- Hours in the day: _____
- Days in the week: _____
- Weekend nights: _____

How much energy should you expend getting in touch with:
- Your BFF: _____
- Your romantic partner: _____
- Your parents: _____

Obvious, the choices you made answering these questions are personal to you. They are choices that communicate your investment in a particular relationship.

People who believe they invest equally in relationships are the happiest.

Commitment

Commitment is your decision to remain in the relationship.
This is a decision not a feeling.

Commitment is a future-oriented approach to relationships. It looks beyond the present feeling—I don't like you right now—to the future—I will like you when I am through being unhappy with your behavior.

Commitment understands that you cannot control your feelings but you can control how you respond to them.

Feelings don't matter much when commitment is the priority.

A strong commitment to a relationship places the relationship above personal, present-time desire.

WELCOME TO
COMMITMENT
ENJOY YOUR STAY!

© Sam72/Shutterstock.com

Trust

Trust is believing in the reliability of the other. When you trust someone, you place your personal well-being in the hands of that person.

Your relationship with your surgeon requires a high level of trust. You trust that your surgeon is competent, reliable, and skilled. You would not have surgery if you didn't have this level of trust.

Trust is earned over time. You don't immediately trust everyone you meet. The great thing about trust in a relationship is that it allows for risk-taking.

The Millionaire Next Door by Thomas J. Stanley and William Danko has something very interesting to say about trust. People become wealthy because they stay married and have a high degree of trust in one another.

- 90% of American millionaires are married couples with an average married life of 38 years and counting.
- These couples put a high premium on the following traits:
  - Unselfishness,
  - caring,
  - forgiving,
  - patient,
  - understanding,
  - disciplined,
  - virtuous,
  - honest,
  - responsible,
  - loving,
  - capable, and
  - supportive.

There is a good deal of trust wrapped up in these characteristics (Stanley and Danko, 2001).

RELATIONAL DIALECTICS

Relationships come pre-packaged with what Baxter and Rawlins call relational dialectics or more commonly inherent tensions (Leslie Baxter 2011; William Rawlins 1992). These tensions spring from the needs, wants, desires, beliefs, attitudes, values, behaviors, and experiences of the people in the relationship. If you want to be successful in your relationships, everyone in them must be aware of the tensions and negotiate about them in good faith. Here they are:

Autonomy or Connection

This dialectic supposes that some people like a lot of freedom and some people don't.

I want my own space. Some people need more space than others. They don't like to feel tied down. They like the idea of being in relationship, but on very loose terms.

I want to be close. Some people need to be close to others all the time. They are not interested in having space. These people like to spend time with their significant other and are not keen on going out or socializing.

Literature, music, and film frequently use this dialectic as a conflict point. If you have seen *Guardians of the Galaxy, vol. 2* you have seen this dialectic at work.

> The sailor said, "Brandy you're a fine girl (a fine girl)
> What a good wife you would be (such a fine girl)
> But my life, my lover, my lady is the sea
> —Eliot Lurie (Looking Glass)

And she wants him to marry her and live with her, but he can't.

Novelty or Predictability

The tension in this dialectic stems from a clash between routine and fear of the same old, same old.

The "I like to do different things all the time" person can be fun to be around because you never know what will happen next. However, this person can be a problem because you never know what will happen next.

The "I like the routine and the comfort and stability that gives me" person gives you stability but can also be kind of boring. The routine is the focus. The lack of spontaneity can cause trouble in a relationship.

Openness or Closedness

This dialectic revolves around self-disclosure. Some people like to talk about everything, others don't.

"I like sharing everything with you." This kind of person may go on at length about everything that happened during the day.

"I don't want to talk about it." This person may think that too much communication is not helpful.

The superhero with the secret identity is in a bind with this dialectic. The superhero can't reveal a secret identity so the loved one can be protected. But, golly, that causes all kinds of relationship trouble.

Your identity is your most valuable possession. Protect it.
—Elastagirl (The Incredibles)

COMMUNICATION CLIMATES

Way back in Chapter 2 we talked about the communication context. We looked at the elements that exist in every context and how those elements affect the communication that happens in the context.

A part of the context we touched on only lightly is something called "the Communication Climate." This climate is created by the people communicating in the context. It consists of the way people treat each other, and how they feel about each other in general and how they feel about each other in a particular communication context.

It is important to understand the climates that are created by those in communication with you so you can understand why and how communication is happening. Clearly, you will be better able to effectively communicate if you accurately assess the climate. Here they are:

CONFIRMING OR DISAGREEING OR DISCONFIRMING

The way we communicate with others tells them how we value them. If we are positive and confirming in our communication, we show we value those with whom we are in relationship. If we disagree, we can still show we value people, we just don't support what they are doing or what they believe. If we are negative and disconfirming, we show we don't value the relationship or those in it. All relationships exist on the confirming or disagreeing or disconfirming continuum. You make the decision where you will communicate along this continuum in each communication situation.

© Popart/Shutterstock.com

There are three types of Confirming or Disagreeing or Disconfirming messages. Remember these are choices you make.

Recognition

You know what if feels like to be ignored, to be considered uninteresting, and to be brushed off.

Your choices of message here are:

Confirming: You exist—I am listening, attentive, and interested. Say more.

Disagreeing: You exist but I am not spending a lot of time here—I am listening but not really interested.

Disconfirming: You don't exist—I am not even looking at you.

© iQoncept/Shutterstock.com

Acknowledgment

Part of being in relationship is acknowledging your commitment, investment, and interconnectedness.
Acknowledging messages are:

Confirming: You matter to me—I care about what you are saying and I am sympathetic. I see you in public and make sure people know we are in relationship.

Disagreeing: You matter but I am not ready to be interested—Talk, but I will half listen. I will briefly chat with you at the party but then you are on your own.

Disconfirming: You don't matter to me—Watch me walk away from you. And I am not going to tell people we are together because I don't want them to know.

The disconfirming acknowledgement message is a staple of literature and film.

© Uber Images/Shutterstock.com

- The secret lovers (Romeo and Juliet, Shakespeare)
- The unknown sibling (Luke and Leia, the Star Wars saga)
- The hidden father (Ego and Peter, Guardians of the Galaxy, vol.2)

These disconfirming messages—the failure to acknowledge the relationship—cause exciting conflicts. That's fine for books and movies, but in real life these messages can destroy relationships.

Endorsement

© Rawpixel.com/Shutterstock.com

You want to be confirming with those you are in relationship with but there are some thing you cannot be made to endorse. You like your friends and love your significant other, but you just don't believe what they do. It would be wrong for you to pretend you do.

Endorsement messages are tricky, then:

Confirming: What you think is true—I am in agreement with you.

Disagreeing: What you think is fine—I think your idea has some merit but I am not totally on board.

Disconfirming: You are wrong—And you will always be wrong, wrong, wrong.

For a little more practice, we can look at some behaviors that we engage in that are generally considered to be disconfirming. You know who you are:

- Don't return phone calls, emails, texts.
- Interrupt every five minutes.
- Give an irrelevant response to the speaker.
- Talk about yourself instead of responding to the message.
- Monologuing. Bad guys in movies do this. It gives the hero time to get away.
- Give vague responses that can mean several different things.

Practice Your C or D or D Climates

Look at this communication situation. Study it a bit and then write a statement that expresses confirmation or disagreement or disconfirmation for each of the three types of messages.

1) Your best friend drops in on you when you're studying for an exam without calling first. After walking in, your friend flops down on the sofa and says, "My parents are acting weird. They're always snapping at each other and seem angry all the time when they're together. I'm really, really worried about what's happening. I think they're getting divorced."

Recognition:

Confirming:

Disagreement:

Disconfirming:

Acknowledgment:

Confirming:

Disagreement:

Disconfirming:

Endorsement:

Confirming:

Disagreement:

Disconfirming

DEFENSIVE OR SUPPORTIVE CLIMATES

Back in 1961, psychologist Jack Gibbs looked at communication climates. That year, he published a study that discusses the defensive or supportive behaviors that exist in relationships. You create these defensive or supportive climates by what behavioral choice you make and how you formulate your message.

© ra2studio/Shutterstock.com

A supportive message is designed to get a supportive response. The more defensive your message, the more likely a defensive response will be. Your choice of course is to be defensive or supportive. The point is that people respond to others with feelings of comfort or discomfort and modify their communication accordingly. Here are Gibb's categories.

Evaluation versus Description

Unless the listener understands the need for evaluation or has asked for it, evaluative messages are viewed as hostile. The listener then becomes defensive. Rather than responding to the content of the message, the listener responds to the emotion the evaluation raised.

© Bruno Passigatti/Shutterstock.com

Descriptive messages take the focus off the person and put it either on the speaker or a behavior. These messages are seen as supportive.

Example: Your boss asks you for a report. You hand it in.

- Evaluation message: You did this wrong.
- Descriptive message: This doesn't have all the information I need.

Certainty versus Provisionalism

Certainty messages are viewed as defensive because they don't leave room for doubt. The listener is reminded that input is not welcome.

Provisional messages leave room for doubt. Input is welcome, leading the listener to believe that the speaker is interested in the listener's ideas.

© Brian A Jackson/Shutterstock.com

Example: You and a friend are debating the important question "Who is better Drake or Meek Mills?"

- Certainty message: Don't confuse me with the fact. I have my mind made up.
- Provisional: I know what I believe but would like your point of view.

Strategy versus Spontaneity

Strategy messages are defensive because they revolve around a hidden agenda. These messages are not honest in any real sense as they hid information or misrepresent information in the pursuit of the speaker's ends.

Spontaneous messages are considered more supportive as they can be more open and honest.

Example: You are late with a project and you want your co-worker's help.

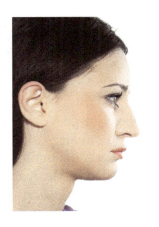

© Vladimir Gjorgiev/Shutterstock.com

- Strategy message: I am in big trouble if I don't get this project done so you need to help me.
- Spontaneous message: Could you help me with this?

Control versus Problem Orientation

Control Oriented messages alert the listener that the listener's needs, wants, and desires are unwelcome. These messages are designed to keep control in the hands of the speaker.

Problem Oriented messages create a climate of cooperation. These messages alert the listener that the listener's needs, wants, and desires are important and valued.

Example: Your significant other comes home with an announcement. (This is a real-life example, by the way.)

- Control Oriented message: I took a new job. We are moving.
- Problem Oriented message: I have been offered a new job but it means we have to move. What do you think?

Neutrality versus Empathy

Neutral messages indicate that you don't care. This is especially true when you are in an empathic listening situation. You may think a neutral message is reassuring, but often it is confused for lack of interest.

Another problem with neutral messages is that they may not accurately reflect what you want.

Empathy messages reflect care for the speaker. They also frankly reflect what you want in a given situation.

Example: You have probably done this a lot. You and your significant other are talking about where to go for dinner. You both say you don't care where you go. But you do. Do I need to tell you how this conversation proceeds?

- Neutral message:
  - ❐ You: I don't care where we go.
  - ❐ SO: Me either. Let's do Italian.
  - ❐ You: No, let's not do that. I am not in the mood. How about Mexican?
  - ❐ SO: No, I'm not interested in Mexican. But I don't really care.

You both care but are unwilling to say so. Try Empathy message. They have less of a chance of fostering a really first-class argument.

■ Empathy message: Let's go where you choose tonight. Next time, I can choose.

Superiority versus Equality

Messages that are formulated to show one's superiority over another are consider defensive. Such messages are used to cut others out completely. They are also used to browbeat people into doing something they don't want to do.

Equality messages are considered supportive because they ask for input from everyone.

Example: You are working in a small group for a class project. One member of the group is being a nuisance. This person is taking over the group and not letting others participate.

■ Superiority message: I'm smarter than you. We will do this my way.
■ Equality message: What is your opinion on how we should handle this?

© Spectral-Design/Shutterstock.com

MAINTAINING RELATIONSHIPS

As of February 2016, the longest-lasting marriage in America was that of John and Anne Betar. They have been married for 83 years. He was 21 and she was 17 when they married.

© Pressmaster/Shutterstock.com

They've said that the secret to their long-lasting union is simple. "We struggled in the beginning, but, luckily, we were content with what we had. It's just important to be content with what you have," John said (Shah, 2016).

How do you build and maintain the relationships you want to keep? By using good interpersonal skills. Here is a checklist that might help. Your answers to these questions will tell you what you need to know to make your relationships better.

Do you take your friends, significant other for granted?

Do you respond to others both verbally and nonverbally? Be aware of and respond to others for granted.

Do you have good command of speaking skills? The better you are able to formulate the message, the better the communication, the better the relationship will be. Can you refrain from saying hurtful or spiteful things?

Do you show contempt of others? This trait is the number one killer of relationships.

Do you use a variety of rhetorical strategies? People like to be addressed as individuals. The extent to which you do this show how much you know about the other and how much you care. You confirm the other's identity when you speak to them as an individual. Don't talk to everyone as if everyone is the same.

Do you have the ability and desire to perceive the world the way the others do? You don't have to understand or like it, just be able to so you know why they behave the way they do.

Do you enjoy the relationship?

Do you tolerate unimportant behaviors? Gum chewing, knuckle-cracking, tuneless humming?

Do you accept that life and people change? That this change is not necessarily a threat?

Do you know what the purpose of the relationship is? Do you both agree on that purpose?

Do you have common goals?

Works Consulted

Anderson, S. *How Many Languages Are There in the World?*, 2017. Retrieved June 02, 2017, from http://www.linguisticsociety.org/content/how-many-languages-are-there-world.

Anderson, S. R. *Languages: A Very Short Introduction*. Oxford: Oxford University Press, 2012.

Baxter, L. A. *Voicing Relationships: A Dialogical Perspective*. Thousand Oaks, CA: Sage, 2011.

Beaton, C. *Why Millennials Are Failing to Shack Up*, October 31, 2015, Retrieved June 02, 2017, from https://www.psychologytoday.com/blog/the-gen-y-guide/201510/why-millennials-are-failing-shack.

Beclown, 2017. Retrieved June 02, 2017, from http://www.urbandictionary.com/define.php?term=beclown.

Bennett, J. *The Beta Marriage: How Millennials Approach "I Do"*, July 25, 2014, Retrieved June 02, 2017, from http://time.com/3024606/millennials-marriage-sex-relationships-hook-ups/.

Berger, C. R., and Calabrese, R. J. "Some Explorations in Initial Interaction and Beyond: Toward a Developmental Theory of Interpersonal Communication." *Human Communication Research*, 1, (1975): 99–112.

Bingham, H. *You Say Potato, I Say Ghoughteighpteau!*, October 07, 2007, Retrieved June 05, 2017, from http://www.dailymail.co.uk/news/article-486294/You-say-potato-I-say-ghoughteighpteau.html.

Cahn, D.D., and Abigail, R.A. *Managing Conflict Through Communication*. 4th ed. Boston, MA: Pearson Education, Inc., 2007.

Chang, L. "Americans Spend an Alarming Amount of Time Checking Social Media on Their Phones." June 13, 2015, Retrieved June 02, 2017, from https://www.digitaltrends.com/mobile/informate-report-social-media-smartphone-use/.

Discover the Story of English More Than 600,000 Words, Over a Thousand Years, 2017. Retrieved June 02, 2017, from http://www.oed.com/view/Entry/16442?redirectedFrom=beclown#eid25792602.

"86 Great Examples of Portmanteau." Retrieved June 05, 2017, from https://www.vappingo.com/word-blog/86-great-examples-of-portmanteau/

Elgin, S. H. *The Language Imperative*. New York, NY: Perseus Books, 2000.

Emanuel, R., Adams, J., Baker, K., Daufin, E. K., Ellington, C., Fitts, E., Himsel, J., Holladay, L., and Okeowo, D. "How College Students Spend Their Time Communicating." *International Journal of Listening* 22 (2008), 13–28.

Gibbs, J. R. "Defensive Communication." *Journal of Communication* 11, no. 3 (1961), 141–8.

How Smell Sends Nonverbal Communication, 2017. Retrieved June 02, 2017, from http://classroom. synonym.com/smell-sends-nonverbal-communication-7361312.html.

Kalinowski, S. and Tapper, M. "The Effects of Seat Location on Exam Grades and Student Perception in an Introductory Biology Class." *Journal of College Science Teaching* (January/February 2007), 54–7.

Kemmer, S. *The Rice University Neologism Data Base*, 2017. Retrieved April 14, 2017, from http:// neologisms.rice.edu/index.php?a=term&d=1&t=2767.

McCorkle, S. and Reese, M. *Personal Conflict Management: Theory and Practice*. Boston: Allyn and Bacon, 2010.

McCroskey, J. C. and McCain, T. A. "The Measurement of Interpersonal Attraction." *Speech Monographs* 41 (1974): 261–6.

Mehrabian, A. *Nonverbal Communication*. Chicago, IL: Aldine-Atherton, 1972.

Mehrabian, A. "Characteristics Attributed to Individuals on the Basis of Their First Names." *Genetic, Social and General Psychology Monographs* 127 (2001): 59–88.

Millennials in Adulthood, March 06, 2014, Retrieved June 02, 2017, from http://www.pewsocialtrends. org/2014/03/07/millennials-in-adulthood/.

Monto, M. and Carey, A. G. "New Standard of Sexual Behavior? Are Claims Associated with the "Hookup Culture" Supported by General Social Survey Data?" *Journal of Sex Research* 51, no. 6 2014: 605–15.

Nordquist, R. *Collocation*, 2016 https://www.thoughtco.com/what-is-collocation-words-1689865.

Pearson, J. C., Nelson. P. E., Titsworth, S., and Harter, L. *Human Communication*. 3rd edn. New York: The McGraw-Hill Co., 2007.

Portmanteau, 2017. Retrieved June 05, 2017, from https://www.merriam-webster.com/dictionary/ portmanteau.

Rawlins, W. K. *Friendship Matters: Communication, Dialectics and the Life Course*. New York: NY: Aldine De Gruyter, 1992.

"Read the Mixed-Up Words." *Physics Forums—The Fusion of Science and Community*, 2017. Retrieved. June 2, 2017.

Rutledge, B. *Cultural Differences—Monochronic versus Polychronic*, August 28, 2011, Retrieved June 02, 2017, from http://thearticulateceo.typepad.com/my-blog/2011/08/cultural-differences-monochronic-versus-polychronic.html.

Shepperd, J., Malone, W., and Sweeney, K. "Exploring Causes of Self-Serving Bias." *Social and Personality Psychology Compass* 2 (2008): 895–908.

Simons, G. F., and Fennig, C. D., eds. Ethnologue: Languages of the World, 20th ed. Dallas, Texas: SIL International, 2017. Online version: http://www.ethnologue.com.

Smith, A., and Anderson, M. "5 Facts About Online Dating." February 29, 2016, Retrieved June 02, 2017, from http://www.pewresearch.org/fact-tank/2016/02/29/5-facts-about-online-dating/.

Snow, B. *This Is Why Millennials Never Want to Grow Up*. December 08, 2016, Retrieved June 02, 2017, from http://www.dailyprincetonian.com/article/2016/12/this-is-why-millennials-never-want-to-grow-up.

Stanley, T. J. *The Millionaire Mind*. Kansas City: Andrews McMeel Publishing, 2001.

Sunnafrank, M. "Predicted Outcome Value During Initial Interactions: A Reformulation of Uncertainty Reduction Theory." *Human Communication Research* 13 (1986): 3–33.

Sunnafrank, M. "Predicted Outcome Values: Just Now and Then?" *Human Communication Research* 13 (1986): 39–40.

Tylee, J. *"Nonverbal Communication: Paralinguistics, Space and Touch,"* Editorial, 2011. education4skills. Com. Retrieved 6 Dec 2011.

Vey, S. and Lichterman, V. *"Listen to This.* Speaking Across the Curriculum," 2017, pp. 1–2. Retrieved June 02, 2017, from http://facultycommons.citytech.cuny.edu/files/FC_SAC-Facts_About_Listening-handout.pdf.

Werthiem, E. G., *The Importance of Effective Communication*. Retrieved June 02, 2017, from http://www.scribd.com/document/69092770/Effective-Communication.

Williams, J. R. "Guidelines for the Use of Multimedia in Instruction," Proceedings of the Human Factors and Ergonomics Society 42nd Annual Meeting, 1998, 1447–1451.

CPSIA information can be obtained
at www.ICGtesting.com
Printed in the USA
LVHW01s2349150817
545002LV00005B/7/P

9 781524 938642